Taking Back The Pen

Resiliency Amidst Life's Predestinated Storyline

An Autobiography

By

Rachel Dawn Fischer

Table of Contents:

Prologue

When you fly as much as I do, you end up sitting next to countless fellow passengers. Some you talk to, some you don't. Some you acknowledge with little more than a nod before you both continue your flight, completely oblivious to each other. Some you remember, most you don't. But some are entirely different. Some change how you see the world and your place in it.

When Rachel sat down next to me on a flight from Atlanta, engaging a fellow passenger was the last thing I wanted. I was on the final leg of a return trip from Australia, barely having slept in over a day. I would happily have zoned out, waiting for the landing gear to touch ground again. But she isn't the kind of girl who lets you zone out when she's sitting next to you. So I gave her my attention. And thank God I did. Yes, at first blush she was remarkably engaging – so much so, that someone not paying attention might have missed telltale signs of darker times in her past. She was full of life and optimism. She even made me laugh about my upcoming divorce. But between her references to adoption as a child, divorce at a very young age, and a nearly fatal accident only a few months earlier, there was clearly much more below the surface of that effervescent personality.

When she mentioned why she had been in Atlanta: a multi-day Christian worship event I was suddenly dubious. I've met too many well-meaning but clueless souls who think they are holy because they mention God and Jesus in every other sentence. I was almost disappointed as I wondered if she was one of them. What I didn't know at the time was that her faith had been tested more than I could imagine. It had done more than endure those trials – it was a large part of the strength that allowed her to conquer them.

The next time you sit next to a woman on a plane, on the bus, or at a restaurant, you may be meeting someone who has been the victim of child abuse, sexual abuse, psychological abuse, and domestic violence. She may be smiling. She may in fact be so beautiful and full of life that she is downright magnetic. But she may be hiding things darker than anything you can imagine.

The book you're holding tells a true story of climbing that mountain – from abuse and suffering that would break the strongest people you know to a love of people and of life few people ever achieve. "Taking Back the Pen" is an apt title. We came up with it while sitting on my kitchen floor after a few cocktails, only months after we met on that plane. It is a tragedy that for many women whose lives mirror the first few chapters of this book, the happy ending you will read does not materialize. They end up either continuing to live in abuse or losing their way somehow. This book is proof that their stories don't have to end the way they so often do.

Everybody has a story. Unless you take the time to ask, you will never know what lies behind a smile. If you meet the author of this book you would never know the horror she has lived through. You would see a beautiful girl who loves her life and her job with more friends then she can count. It's not that she's hiding her past; she's simply not letting it define her. If you are experiencing abuse, poverty, depression, or any of the other troubles that befall people making their way in the world, these pages will hopefully speak to you. Even if you're not, they contain a story that will touch and inspire you to help others.

After all, the next time you sit on a plane, there may be a story still being written sitting next to you.

Introduction

The thought was raised by a former English professor whom I highly respect; would it be pointless to write a book that may have already been written before, or is it selfish not to? To share the wisdom and insight that you were chosen to live for in life, to write about the things that gave your life purpose - would it be selfish to write it, or would it be selfish to keep the story hidden? On the other hand, if you did not write that book would then it be considered selfish to your potential readers?

All my life I have been told that I need to write a book. I tossed the idea around for many years. As events built up in my life and climaxes plummeted, I wondered if I would be writing the book for a particular audience or if I would be writing it for myself. It can now be verified that it is cathartic to get your thoughts and experience down on paper. So to say I wrote the book for myself is part of the motivation. I've often wondered, how could it be cleansing for a person to pick up my book, read my story and feel better about himself? After pondering the options, I decided that if only one person would be affected for the better by reading my book, than that would mean that at least two people were affected by it and therefore the book would be worth writing.

I find that writing a book does not mean to just recall life events and put them on paper. That would be considered journaling. I've learned that to write a book means to write intentionally. It's debatable whether or not this can cause more harm than good on a personal level for the writer. I went through many sleepless nights tossing and turning after recalling feelings and events surrounding the events I have written about. The pain of living the events is brought back to the light as the story is written down on paper. The part that hurts the most is the memory of the hurt sustained through it all and acknowledging the scars still present. The part that makes it tolerable is being able to smile and keep my chin up, knowing that I'm still here to write about it. There were many points along the way where ending my life seemed like a better option than going on in misery, let alone waiting around to tell people about my trials.

It's hard to write a book like this one without feeling like you're throwing people under the bus by exposing things they have done to you and put you through. Part of the cleansing and teaching aspect from writing a book comes from the fact that you have learned to settle and make peace with these people and the situations that surround them. It is hard to bring light to these events again, but in order for these lessons to be learned from by the reader, issues need to be resurfaced, admitted and faced. For many years I ignored all the problems that came my way. I would store things away and just live life as though those things had never happened. I learned to compartmentalize very well. I had to come to the realization that I will never learn from trials and mistakes if I deny their existence altogether. These events in my story happened, and they are real. You will be very disturbed by some of the things you are about to read. Some of the details are fairly graphic. Believe me, they were as difficult for me to write as they are for you to read. As a growing, learning young girl I was confused about the things happening to me. I look back and realize that I was chosen for this path I am writing about. At the same time, it is rewarding to see that the hurts I faced were all for a purpose. It was all a lesson, both for me and, as I write my book now at the age of 24, I understand that it was also for my potential readers. Even if the hurt and challenges I faced only happened so that you could be reading this book right now, it was worth struggling through them.

We all have pain and sorrow and we all could tell a story, but how many people actually write their book? How many people were supposed to write a book but didn't? How many stories have been covered up by other stories that don't matter? Does any story really matter? I believe so. A person who writes a book needs to be prompted to do so, and it is usually for a specific reason. The fact that you are reading this tells me that you are either looking for answers, maybe answers from my story that you feel may go along with how you are feeling in your situation. You may be glad that this story was put out there to share a story similar to yours, and this may give you hope that your story will matter as well. This book may inspire you to write your own and I hope it does. Whatever the case, keep in mind that we all matter and in some way our stories all connect and our situations overlap. We need to open our eyes to let our minds figure things out so that our hearts can finally feel. Some people make a choice to think deeper. Some people don't live life any other way. I hope this book raises awareness to people that life goes deeper and carries on to different levels behind closed doors that we don't always want to see.

As I set out to write this book, I knew that there would be people to whom this book would impact. This is not a page to thank but rather acknowledge those that played a part in my story. There are people this book will offend; people may be shocked at its content. There are people who will be outraged at the things I have put in about my past. The people I have written about are the people who shaped my story and those are the people who have made me into the person I am today. Without them, this book would have no base. That may be a "Thank you" but it may also be an "I'm sorry." In writing this book the intent is solely to change or impact the way people may view life and to think from a different perspective. As you see in the title, this book will hit on many points of abandonment and struggles in my past. These events were driven by the life I was born into and the influences of other people on my life's course. But the key to understanding this book is to grasp that I was able to grab ahold of the pen and write my own ending.

Chapter 1

The Adoption

There I sat, a four-year-old girl, in a dark room filled with heroin needles, lighters and walls covered in blood. As I heard the sirens and shouts, confusion and chaos, I knew that something was about to happen and things were about to change. I heard voices on megaphones coming from outside in the front yard letting us know the house was surrounded. The door was kicked open and the raid began. As my 10-year-old brother Brian tried to hide me in a closet, a tall, thin, dark haired female social worker came between us and took me from his arms. Our mom lay drunk and full of heroin on the couch not able to comprehend what was going on in her own living room. The police stood around and went in and out of rooms. There were many arrests made that day. The people who were always hanging around in the house with us were finally taken into custody and I was taken down the front steps by a police officer. As they put me in the social worker's vehicle, I kicked the dashboard of her car. I was screaming to be let out. I turned and looked through the back window as we drove away. I saw my mom stumbling down the steps confused and finally becoming aware that I was being taken away. I watched her being pulled back in and handcuffed by a police officer. My brother got out of the arms of the other social worker and chased the car down the road until the police officer grabbed him and held him back. That was the last time I saw my brother Brian until I was 6 years old. That is one of the earliest memories I have. That moment is one of the recurring dreams and flashbacks I suffer with today.

That day I was taken to the Department of Social Services. I stayed in that facility for a few weeks until a foster home was found for me. Being so young it is hard to recall the specific events surrounding my time in the foster care system. I can just remember different children that were my playmates and adults being around us showing us how to clean up our toys in the common areas. What I did know was that none of these children were my brother so I was very hostile toward the children there. I remember being put in time out a lot for how I treated the other children. I was a troubled child. I can see why I struggle with temperament issues today. I remember the day that they brought the prospective family over to me. The social worker told me that these people wanted to bring me to their home with other brothers and sisters to play with and that they would love me and take care of me. I remember thinking such a naïve thought that being in a home with fewer children than I currently was around would give me access to more toys that I wouldn't have to share.

When the family walked toward me I saw a seemingly happy husband and wife. I couldn't care less about the story that went with them. All I wanted was someone to love me and to give me a home and I wanted a chance to get out of there to see my brother Brian again. I walked to the gated window with the social worker that was in charge of my case. The new parents were standing on the other side of the window completing their paperwork.

All I could think of is that this may mean that I may get to see my brother again once I got free from that place. I had no idea what kind of situation I was getting into, nor did they. These parents that I went home with had 6 other children at home and I was the last child they brought home. They had chosen to foster and adopt only special needs children. I was the 7th special needs child they had chosen. I was deemed special needs because I was born to a mother who did drugs while pregnant with me. I had attachment disorder and night terrors and I was hard to control. The anger outbursts I had towards the other children deemed me to be a special needs child as well.

I lived with this family for the next year and had many meetings with social workers and several evaluations by psychologists. The choice was made for this family to keep me. At the age of five years old there was a court date and I was officially adopted into this family. The next two years were strange and full of experience. There were various days of visits at the court house from my biological mother, supervised of course, and by the time I turned 6 my biological father was allowed to bring my biological brother to visit me at my adopted parents' house. My life was complete as long as my brother Brian was coming to play with me and to be a part of my life again.

At that time in my life I went by another name, a name given at birth, my first alias. My name at that time was Melissa. My biological brother Brian would call me Lisa. To this day the people in my community who knew me from the time I was adopted still call me by my first given name. It is weird to hear that name spoken. It is surreal. It reminds me of a distant past. It is hard to explain to people today why my name was changed. It is the first question people ask when they find out about it. My new adopted parents were trying to protect me from my biological mother. Communication with her was cut off after she was taken back to prison. I still turn my head every time I hear someone say Melissa. That was my name. That was who I was. It is hard to undergo a name change like that. At such a young age, it was hard to understand. It led to me questioning things later in life about who I really am. I struggle enough with figuring out who my "real family" is let alone who I am and what my name really is. To me, I feel more comfortable with Melissa. That is who I really am. Legally my name is now Rachel. Each time I write it or say it, I still feel as though I am hiding a part of myself. I met a man on a plane recently and when he asked me my name he looked at me funny when I told him that my name was

Rachel. He told me that name didn't suit me and he asked if I ever went by another name. When I explained to him that it used to be Melissa, he smiled and told me that was the name that suited me. It is hard for me to go back and forth from the people who knew me as Melissa, who still use that name while talking to me, and then the people in my later years call me Rachel. It throws me back and forth and I struggle with what my name really should be.

By the time I turned 7, one of my older adopted sisters had run away from home and no one has seen her still to this day. I didn't blame her. If I had the means and understanding I would have run away from the situation we were in, too. It wasn't fun. It wasn't fair. It was more uncomfortable than anything. Two years after I lived there, the two oldest twin brothers moved out at age 18 to try and find their own biological family. I was left in this new home with two brothers and a sister. They were each severely mentally disabled. The older sister had a traumatic brain injury from a car accident before she was adopted into this new family. The other two brothers were drug babies as well and the oldest of the two had fetal alcohol syndrome and was his own mess of a person.

As the months passed, I noticed my adopted mother being gone more and more and my adopted father was always gone at work. I thought maybe she was out looking for her other daughter that had run away. That is the only thing that made sense in my mind at the time. I would try to help in my own way by watching out the windows everyday waiting for her to come back home. Finally the answer came to why she was always gone. That year I was told by my adopted mother that she was going to leave my adopted father and she was going to be moving into another house. She told me that when I saw the judge at the next court hearing I needed to tell him that I did not want to stay with my adopted father and the rest of the children but that I wanted to move in with her. I was confused and had no idea what was going on. My adopted father, on the other hand, was telling me to tell the judge that I wanted to stay there with him and the other children. She would tell me terrible things about my adopted father. She told me that he never spent time with her because he didn't love her and that he didn't spend time with me because he didn't love me either. She wanted me to choose her side. At 7 years old I didn't understand why my adopted father didn't love us. It made sense in a way because he was always working. I had started to believe her.

I remember my adopted mother coming to the house while my dad was at work and taking boxes of things to her van. She let me help her carry things out. She said she was giving them to families in need. I figured that I was helping her do something good. I didn't understand at the time what she had me doing. Looking back I see that she was taking things to her new trailer. Her and her boyfriend were moving into a local trailer park. She had me helping her with it not knowing what was going on. When I found out later in life, I struggled with anger towards her for a long time after I found out what I helped her accomplish. I blamed myself for the hurt that my adopted father faced through the divorce because I felt like I helped her hurt him.

On the day of the court hearing to determine who would get custody of me, I remember standing in front of the judge and saying that I wanted to stay with my dad. I didn't understand at the time why I was saying that but I knew that my dad had told me to say it for a reason. I can clearly remember the hurt in his face that he carried around with him. It that was the sad look of someone that needed help but was too afraid to ask. I had a sense of helping people even then so I knew that staying with him was the only thing I was capable of doing to help him. I remember the look of anger in my adopted mother's eyes when I made the decision and I didn't understand her reaction. I thought she was mad at me. It made me feel like the divorce was all happening because of me.

Now that I am older I look back at the situation having learned the truth about what was going on. My adopted mother was having an affair for 6 years during the adoptions. Her plan was to adopt until she got the daughter that she always wanted. She told me that she waited years for me. After adopting me she planned on taking me with her and running off with the man she had the affair with. I was angry at first after finding this out and I felt resentment towards her for a long time. I felt bad for my adopted father because he was married to a woman he loved who had always wanted children. He personally never wanted children. He was willing to adopt us 7 children because he loved her and wanted his wife to be happy. He worked 16 hours a day to support us all, not knowing that at the same time she was planning her own life on the side. She claims she left him because he was never around because he worked too much, that she was lonely and wanted a new family and a man to love her. In his defense the children she adopted were the reason he had to be gone to work so much. Her actions were not justified and in no case do I believe that an affair should ever be justified. I do see that my father worked a lot and I understand now that it wasn't his choice to work so much but in order to support us he didn't have any other option.

I lived with my adopted father and two special needs brothers and one special needs sister for several years after my adopted mother left. Our adopted father worked all the time so we basically raised ourselves. We had visitation days with our mother. She had to come to our house when she wanted to see us because the man she lived with had five kids of his own and he didn't want us coming to their trailer. Mondays were the days she would visit. The visitations I looked forward to were from my biological father and brother Brian. They would come to visit me at my adopted father's house twice a week and my biological brother would stay a couple days at a time with us. I was content just being able to spend time with Brian. To this day I am grateful for those days and those moments I shared with him. When I was 9, my adopted sister ended up moving out when she got married to another special needs man. My adopted mother got married to the man she was having an affair with when I was 9, as well. I was left in the house with two brothers. Those days spent with them were not easy for me as a young girl. I still wonder if I can blame the two of them for the things they did to me during that time or if their disabilities leave them blameless. Either way, I struggled for a long time with the difficulty of forgiving them. I will get into further details about what they put me through later in the book.

After my adopted parents' divorce, my adopted dad would leave for work and I would be left with the two special needs brothers that were 6 and 10 years older than me. I went through years of physical and sexual abuse with the brothers as my dad went off to work. It got to the point where they would bring the neighbor boys over to "play" the games with me as well. As a little girl I didn't understand what was going on and what was normal and right or wrong. I subdued those thoughts that came back through the years until recent years. I have finally been able to emotionally face the challenges I went through. The sickness in my stomach radiates to my heart and I feel broken, abused and poisoned to this day. I grew up thinking that the things that were happening to me were just normal things that all the other girls my age went through. The older brother is now running around with the circus after having two children with mentally handicapped women from our neighborhood and leaving the state. I haven't heard from him in years and now that I am finally facing what it was he did to me, I choose never to contact him again even if he does come back around. There is no telling what lies in the mind of someone like that. When my adopted mother's new husband finally let us come visit their trailer, I would stay for weekends with them in the trailer park. I made many friends there that told me they faced a lot of the same challenges in life that I went through. I finally had people my age to relate to. People at school made fun of me when I would stay there and the other girls called me trailer trash. They didn't understand what I went through and I could care less what they thought because being in the trailer park, I found friends who hurt in the same way I did. I felt a sense of belonging there.

To this day I have never told my adopted father the things that happened to me while he was away at work because I don't want him to blame himself for never being around. I don't blame my adopted father for the things that happened to me. The only reason he was never there is because he had to work two jobs to support the kids that he had adopted for the wife who he thought was going to help raise them. I know so many people today that suppress the hurtful thoughts like I did. People bury the feelings and emotions that go along with sexual abuse and they pretend like it never happened. I learned that unless you deal with the emotions you are burying, they will eat you from the inside out. It is painful and embarrassing to admit that these things happened. I hated bringing them up when entering recent relationships but if I didn't bring them out into the open I would never be able to live a normal life. The person you end up spending your life with needs to know the trials you have faced so that they will understand when you have breakdowns and panic attacks at random times. The person you choose to spend your life with should know you better than yourself. You can't get help unless you admit that you are in need. I am the last person to ask for help, but when it comes to issues of deep emotion, we all need someone who can pick us up from our hardest falls.

Chapter 2

The Foster Family Struggles

Through the post-divorce years and the abuse I went through in my adopted home, the one thing I can look back on as a strong positive influence was that my adopted father kept us in a local church. This was a very conservative Baptist church with a strict, legalistic approach that I now see as a hindrance to my spiritual life. At the time, though, the rules and strong religion were what I needed. We would get rides from the church van and go to church twice a week and do camps and church programs. I looked forward to it. It was my escape. The families at the church were sympathetic to our situation. They would bring us food and donate clothes to us. On Sundays, different families in the church would take turns taking me and my two brothers home in between morning and evening church services. We would get fed full meals and we would see how other families lived. It was inspiring to see that there were families who sat together at meals, asked about homework and had parents that helped them out. It was good to see that the despair we faced at home was not the same in all families. It gave me a sense of hope. To see structure of mothers, fathers children and pets, it all seemed so close, yet so far away.

The church gave us structure. For me personally I learned my morals, wisdom and values. Being a part of that religion taught me how to think, how to love and how to care. I would go away to church camps and be around other kids and teens and I would share my story and hear other stories and be inspired. It showed me at a young age that I wasn't necessarily alone in a lot of the struggles I faced. I made friends with people all over the state of Michigan who shared some of the same hurt as I did. Those weeks away at camp inspired me to learn others' stories, to be able to relate and to be able to help. I was always a helper. I had to be strong. I had to sustain myself all the time so it made me grow up faster than most. I found myself counseling others my age at an early phase of my life. What I noticed was the camp counselors that were assigned to a group of girls would hear our stories and have no wisdom to give us. They had never felt the hurt before and they didn't understand the pain. As I would get advice from people who knew nothing about the trials I faced, all I could think is that I needed to use my trials someday to help others because I would actually understand. Eventually when I grew up I was able to become a camp counselor and utilize my experiences to help others. Even to this day I still counsel and mentor others who struggle with the same trials I faced.

Another factor that gave me structure in those hard days was that my dad had put me into a private Christian school starting in 6th grade after a recommendation from a family at the church. The other brothers were in a special education program and didn't test high enough to get into the school, so I was the only child in my home that got to attend the private school. There was personal attention from teachers at this small school, yet there were strict rules to follow. The girls and boys were separated in almost every situation. I had to wear skirts below my knees and no clothing with logos was allowed. I could not watch movies or listen to any type of music other than church hymnals. There were many strict rules but it was all for the best. Many different students in great family situations surrounded me, and it helped to see normalcies in their families.

Most of my fellow students were stuck up and never even had a thought of letting me into their private cliques. I was an outsider. I didn't fit in any particular group. I was the center of ridicule, and I was the girl who got made fun of for what I wore and the way I looked. It was a give and take feeling to be a part of a private school because I struggled with jealousy many times. All the girls had the latest Hollister and American Eagle clothing. I never had anything that was considered "in style." All the clothes I wore were handed down from friends at the trailer park or given to me from women at church. I would see other students coming in with lunches made by their mothers and I would be eating candy bars and a soda from the snack shop because that's all I could afford with the $2 a day my adopted dad gave me for lunch. We never had food in the house to bring.

Regardless of those downfalls, I credit the higher education I received for the education and career I eventually attained. I did not like the rules the school had or the legalism that went along with it. I rebelled in many ways, but looking back I can see the benefit to it. I stayed active in sports and I went on mission trips with the school and church to different countries and cities to serve a higher purpose. I learned about different cultures. I opened my mind and I removed myself from the box I was in that tried to limit my future. I stepped out of that box. I learned early that the only person that will ever help to better a person is himself. I saw that unless I moved forward no one would walk forward for me, and if I didn't move then I would be stuck and alone. I stayed active. I involved myself in sports. I stayed away from my house as much as possible. I made my life brighter. I held to the faith that I was taught and I kept moving onward and upward.

Looking back at that situation, it seemed so devastating at the time to not fit in to the popular crowd. I remember how bad I felt about not having the name brand clothing. I did everything I could to try to wear the nice clothes that all the other girls were wearing. I remember trying to save up my money for an American Eagle jacket so that all the other kids would think I was as cool as they were. When I graduated and started working more I finally had enough money to buy the clothing I wanted. The first chance I got, I went to the mall and updated my wardrobe with the latest brands and styles. After a while I looked around and realized that I had spent a lot of money on clothing. I also realized, that I was only doing this for myself. The people that I wanted to impress were not even in my circle of friends anymore. I realized I would never see the people I was in middle school and high school with ever again. Then I realized that the brands I strived to get meant nothing in the bigger picture of life. The big excitement about wearing brands was temporary during school. Now that I am older, I realize that no one cares what brands you wear. I learned that the little things that seem huge at the time are just fleeting ideas that no one cares about long term. If I would have known then what I know now about the reality of society and what is really important in life, I would have been a happier teenager. I also would have had more self-confidence which would have helped my case out quite a bit. I learned that lesson in time, but I found that it is very common for people at that age to seek to attain the name brand fads in order to fit in. That just may be a phase that all young people have to face on their own. All I can say is that one day you will realize what really matters and what doesn't.

Chapter 3

Remarriage

I was 12 years old. I was dealing with preparing to go to high school and all the emotions that come along with becoming a teenager and figuring out who you are. As if things weren't hard enough as it was, on the home front I would get calls coming in from a girl named, "Christina from class". As my dad handed me the phone I would walk around the corner and tuck the coiled phone cord into my door as I shut it and hid to prepare myself for the upcoming conversations. The first time I got the phone call the caller told me to speak quietly and not let anyone know who was really calling me. When she revealed herself I found that the caller was my biological mother calling me from Florida State Prison. As I spoke on the phone with my biological mother, I didn't quite understand why I had to keep her a secret and didn't comprehend why she didn't want anyone to know she was calling me. She still called me Melissa. She would ask me if I got her letters and why I never wrote back. I told her that I didn't even know that she was writing to me. The answer was summed up in the fact that she had to disguise who she was to call me because my adopted father was trying to protect me from her. He would read and throw away the letters so that I didn't know she was trying to reach me. My adopted parents tried to protect me from her, but they were unsuccessful. She would tell me stories about my childhood and about the times with my brother and about her pregnancy with me. She told me the traumatic stories she went through being around a group of bikers that included my biological father, which ultimately led to two of her pregnancies. She would express her love for me and her deep apologies for being in prison away from me. She told me her plans to get me back. She told me that she would save me from the situation I was in and take my brother and I somewhere where we could all become a family again. She tried to teach me over the phone how to feel, how to live and how to think. She explained to me the things she did to get herself into prison. Her list of offenses included things such as grand theft auto and forgery, check fraud, and drug sales. She would try to tell me the mistakes she made that got her caught and gave me the proper ways to follow through with the situations so I could follow in her footsteps and be successful as a criminal.

Those were emotional days for me. Hanging up the phone and knowing that there was someone who possibly loved me more than the people I was living with gave me a sense of hope. Despite who she was and the hopelessness of the life she was living, it still made me dream. I passed the thoughts through my head of the things she told me to try to accomplish that she failed at. I figured that since it was in my blood someday I would end up being as powerful and manipulative as she was. I thought maybe I would get caught doing so and be able to go to the prison she was in so I could finally be with my real mom.

The only thing that gave me hope was my biological brother Brian. The days that he came to visit with me made me feel a part of something. He was the only one I had in my life that was truly my flesh and blood. Brian was the one person I could call mine. He made me feel safe. We shared the same mother, the same father, the same eyes and the same heart. We loved each other more than anything and I cherished him more than anything. He looked after me and promised to always protect me and that he would never let anyone hurt me. He was my safety net - the only one who I knew really loved me because we were true family. Brian cared about me more than he cared about himself. He would have sacrificed his life for me. I was his purpose in life. He was MY big brother and I was HIS Melissa.

Through the years after the divorce of my adopted parents, while we were growing up, my adopted father was dating different women. Of course, as children we protected our dad and we terrorized the new women coming around because we didn't want anyone else to get our dad. No child wants their parents to get remarried after a divorce. It is a fine line that the parents walk to show love to their kids and at the same time try and build love in their own life. That year my adopted father met another woman that he started bringing around the house more than he used to bring the others around. She was stubborn and didn't respond to us trying to scare her away. She stuck with him. Six months later they were married. I can still remember having a talk with my dad a month before the wedding telling him that we didn't want him to marry this woman because of the things she said and did to us while he was away. I can still remember her telling me that I was not even his blood and that he would always choose her over any of us because we were going to be out of his life soon anyway.

That year spawned a whole new chapter of my life. This woman had five children of her own. My stepmother's children put the total number of my brothers and sisters to 22. There were 7 adopted siblings from my adopted parents when they were together. There were five stepsiblings on my adopted mother's side from the new man she married that he already had from a previous marriage. There were now five stepsiblings on my new stepmothers side and five on my biological side. This woman was great for my adopted father in the light of him being lonely after my mom divorced him. He now had a companion. Looking at it that way I can understand the need for him to have a spouse whether we as his children liked the woman he chose or not, so that he has someone to take care of him when he ages. In that light I am okay with her being a part of his life. At that time in my life, for her and I and my two brothers who were still in the house, it was a detrimental situation.

That year things started going downhill fast. Any attention I was aiming to get from my dad was taken away. I was no longer allowed to call him at work to talk to him about my day. I was no longer able to go to dinner with him anymore by myself. When he came home he went upstairs to the room they shared and she would not let us come up to see him anymore. We couldn't even talk to him up the stairs. In my eyes, she took my dad away from me. Looking back now I understand her side and her hurt. She faced struggles with her ex husband that made her cling so tight to my dad that she would keep him from his own children. I can understand that as a woman now. But it was not right. At the time, I was just a young girl and all I saw was abandonment and betrayal. How she handled it was her coping mechanism but the way she coped hurt his children and was unjustifiable.

Those next years living with this new stepmother were crazy to say the least. At this point the oldest brother had moved away to work with the circus. That left my other mentally handicapped brother and me in the house. He lived with the mind capacity of a 7 year old when he was 20 years old. Things happened to me during that time that no one should ever even wish upon their worst enemy. Her sons from her previous marriage would come to visit on occasion. They were abusive both physically and verbally. I would make it a point to be away from the house whenever they came to visit. She removed all the food from the house and locked it in the garage. She took the TV away and made the living room off limits to us. She would mandate that my special needs brother and I stay in our rooms during the day. She would leave out bowls of cereal on top of the fridge for the morning meal times. The bathroom door was taken off so we couldn't even go to the bathroom or shower in private. She limited our shower times to two minutes and would turn the hot water off at that time limit. She removed our clothes from our rooms, put them in the garage and gave us two outfits to wear for the week. The clothing situation was the hardest for me because in the Christian school I went to all the other girls had the latest clothing and had everything they wanted given to them. I chose to wear all black all the time so that no one would notice that I was wearing the same clothes everyday. I went along with the theme and called myself a Goth. I started listening to heavy metal music and would associate myself with the Goths and Punks. She would not let us do our laundry and would not buy us shampoo, soap for the shower, toothpaste or other necessities. My father was a workaholic and continued going on with life as usual. He had no idea what was going on at home because he was never home and didn't pay any attention to the complaints I would bring to him. I was never allowed to be alone with him to get a chance to tell him about what she did to us when he wasn't around.

At this point, at age 12, I knew that I was going to have to get a job to make money to feed my brother and myself. I walked down the street to a local insurance agency and I talked to the office manager. I asked her if I could clean the office bathrooms for her as a side job. The manager laughed and told me that pretty girls don't clean bathrooms, so she hired me as a paper filer instead. I began to work in the back of the office for two hours a day after school. The office was only a mile down the street so I could walk to and from work everyday. I made less than minimum wage but it was enough for me to buy food for my brother and me. It was hard emotionally for me to take care of the adopted brother that took part in sexually abusing me with the older adopted brother and their friends when I was younger. There was an internal conflict I faced with that situation. I had to move past that and I kept in mind that he didn't have the mind capacity to understand right and wrong and that he probably didn't do those things to hurt me. I maintained strength to look past that and actively forgive him for the awkward situations he put me in and I made sure he was taken care of and that he had food to eat. I was finally able to buy my lunches at school. I was able to stop at the CVS that was on my walk home from the insurance agency to buy laundry detergent, shampoo and toothpaste for us. I had to hide it because when I left it out she would empty the containers into the garbage and wish me good luck in buying more. She started searching my room and confiscating things. I had built a fort out back in the woods behind my house that I would hide supplies in to counteract that situation. The things she did were unheard of but I fought back and I became strong-willed due to it. I had to learn to think wisely and to be crafty.

To give you an example of how desperate and naive my special needs brother was, I will tell you about a story when he was arrested. He had gone down our street late one night and broke into an eyeglass store at the end of our street. He broke into the back door of this building and the alarms went off. The police found him while he was walking back towards our house. In the place he broke into, he left the money in the cash register. What he stole allowed the police to realize they were dealing with a situation less severe than it seemed. They came to our house and told my adopted dad that they found the place broken into with the money left where it was. He had emptied the candy bowl from the front desk and put it all in his pockets. He took the cans of pop from the break room fridge and hid them in his jacket pockets. The police asked him why he broke in and left the money, and all he could say was that he was hungry. I told my dad that he needed to take a look at the bigger picture because something was obviously wrong with the way he and I were being taken care of while he was away at work.

I was on the perfect attendance list at school. Going to a private school there was no bus system so I had to be driven to and from school each day. Lucky for me there were other families that lived close who were able to drive me to and from school every day. During the last week of the perfect attendance contest, my stepmother purposefully drove me to school two hours late and laughed at me the whole way as I looked out the window and cried because I lost my chance at getting the perfect attendance award that I had looked forward to getting. I can still hear her yelling out the window at me as she pulled away from the school "too bad Rach. Maybe next year." I decided that day that I was not going to put up with that anymore. I began to rebel and take a stand for my brother and myself. This new attitude led to many fights and verbal assaults on both ends. I became very difficult to live with. I became very harmful with my words and I learned to speak out people's weaknesses as a weapon. It was the only way I knew to defend myself. I entered into a state of rebellion against school, church, parents and friends. I was at a breaking point where nothing was fair and nothing made sense. She kept telling me that my dad would choose her over me any day and I grew to believe it after seeing his lack of reaction to later events. Eventually the day did come when he chose her over me when he decided to send me away to my adopted mother's house. I will write more about that later in the book. The day that happened was the day life began to break down further. My thoughts darkened and depression kicked in. Suicide looked like the best option for me. I tried to overdose on medications but it just left me sick and in pain. I would cut my wrists and the inside of my legs because I wanted to feel the pain. The day that I decided that I needed to make a choice to end my life the right way was the day I asked my father to take me to a facility where I could get help, otherwise I would not be alive when they found me in the morning. I was taken to a psych facility that day and I started to get my thinking under control.

The woman my dad married may have been a good wife for him but she was not healthy for me. We did not get along at all, and she did not treat me well in the least. Although she was not good for me, and as much as I dislike her, I had to realize that she was a good thing for my adopted father. He was lonely and hurting. He needed a lover in his life. I looked at women coming into his life as intruders. I didn't understand at the time that an individual's love interest, becomes more important than secondary relationships. I see that my dad was in love and he needed to get remarried again in order to be healthy himself. I now understand from experience that it is very rare for children to approve of any stepparent that comes into their separated parents' lives. My stepmother may have been a harmful relationship to me, and that is something I personally have to deal with and work through. Not all stepparents are abusive and I realize that. I now accept the fact that a parent is an individual person and has his or her own needs as well, so a stepparent coming in is a good thing for them, and it is selfish to disapprove of their new love. I am not giving approval of the way she treated her stepchildren, because it was not right, and I am not saying that the anger I retaliated back towards her was okay either. I am saying that in a healthy situation, a stepparent is a good thing for the parent that has finally found a new love. This is VERY hard for any child to grasp, and the acceptance will come in time. The bottom line is that the stepparent will NEVER take the place of the original parent, but in healthy situations, they should still be adopted into the family as a part of the new picture.

Chapter 4

Brian's Fate

My 13th birthday party was a day I will not forget. As I leaned over to blow my candles out, I heard a knock. I looked over at the back door and saw my biological brother Brian walking in. I stopped and ran to him and hugged him so tightly. I was so thankful he was there. He had not been coming around much that year due to my stepmother keeping him away and my adopted father asked him and my biological father to come around less. When Brian came to visit, it was always in secret or late at night when no one knew.

That day my stepmother and adopted father told me to go back to my cake and took Brian outside to talk in the garage. When they walked back in without him and the smoke of my candles filled the air I ran to the driveway to see him angrily pulling away. I didn't understand why he would leave my party. He had just arrived and he didn't even say goodbye. I found out that my parents had told him that he was not allowed in the house ever again and that he was not allowed to see me until he quit the drugs he was taking and got his life back on track. Granted, he did live with my biological father who was a biker and they lived a rough lifestyle. Brian had dropped out of high school, had gotten involved with the wrong crowd, and was into drugs. In his defense he was only 19 years old and that was the only life he knew. If the social worker had not taken me away the night my mom's house was raided, then I would have grown up in the same lifestyle as he was stuck living in. I understand the intent of my adopted father making him leave now but at the time it did not seem fair. I spent the rest of that night locked in my bedroom and I refused to speak to anyone else that was at my party. I had slid my arm across the table that my cake was on casting all of my gifts and everything on the table onto the floor. That was the angriest I had been in a long time. Since this event in my life, I have started evading my birthday each year. Most people avoid birthdays because of the age factor. I never realized why I was not fond of my birthday until a recent discussion with a psychologist. When she brought me back to the scene where I saw my brother last, it was at my birthday. It finally hit me. That day on my 13th birthday I ran from my own party after Brian left. What happened the following year fixed the distain for my own birthday into my mind. Subconsciously I have harbored this distain for my birthday unaware of the deeper emotional tie that surrounded the event.

That year after Brian's final visit was one of the hardest of my teenage years. The struggles grew between my stepmother and I. I began to fade to a darker place in my life than I had already gotten into. I hadn't heard from my brother in months and I grew to resent my parents for scaring him away. I felt he no longer loved me and I started to feel that I had no one again. I got into the punk lifestyle. I would cross my arms in class and at church. I would smart off to people and I didn't care who I was hurting. I would do things like covering my jeans in duct tape and safety pins to add to the punk phase I was in. This was the summer before my sophomore year of high school. In the meantime while I was in this phase of anger and rebellion, I found out later that Brian had left my birthday that day and told my biological father that he could not bear to lose me in his life and that he was going to do everything he could to show my parents that he was changed and worthy to be a part of my life again. Brian had gone back that year and gotten his GED. He had gotten into rehab and gotten clean from drugs and was still working on quitting alcohol. He started a job doing roofing and had started the process of buying a house. He told everyone each month that he was closer to his goal of getting his sister back. Brian had turned his life around. He had become a new person because he loved me enough to do anything to see me again and to be a part of my life to watch me grow. His goal in life had changed for me. I was his reason for becoming a better person. I had no idea that he was doing these things at the time. I just thought that he didn't want to see me anymore.

In the midst of my depression, my adopted mother told me to get into her car one day to take a drive because we had somewhere we needed to go and that it was a surprise. She and my adopted father drove me to a building in Detroit where there were hundreds of motorcycles outside. I had no idea what was going on. As I walked inside, I was surrounded by men in leather jackets. They all looked at me with sympathetic glances. I saw my biological father walk toward me in tears. That hug was the longest hug in my life. He hugged me and didn't let go for several moments. I looked around at hundreds of bikers and many sad faces and when I asked what was going on they led me to the casket in the funeral home. As I looked down I saw my brother Brian lying in the casket holding a single rose. I fell back and screamed. One of the bikers grabbed me from behind and held me tightly. My heart sank and the anguish and anger and confusion filled me. I turned to run and my biological father grabbed me and helped me fall to the ground in front of the casket as I wept. I asked so many questions. I didn't understand. There were so many emotions I felt that first hour. I had anger towards my parents and anger towards my brother. I felt the devastation of losing him and still asked myself the question of whether this was real or not. As I sat down in the front row still in shock, Brian's friends came forward to hug me and tell me the stories of Brian and what I meant to him and the plans he had in his life. Tears fall even as I write this story because there is no way for me to look back on this day and not cry. There are two main traumatic incidents that I have flashbacks to. The first is the day I was taken away during the raid when my brother chased the car, and the other is the day I looked down at my brother's body in the casket.

My biological father kept telling me that I didn't need to worry because he believed in reincarnation and told me that Brian was still somewhere among us. That was not encouraging to me because that was not my belief. I knew in my heart that Brian was gone and was never coming back. I didn't have the same comfort that my father did within his religion. That day at the funeral I met my biological aunts, uncles, and grandparents of Brian and I. That day I also I met my biological sister for the first time. She was a half sister I didn't even know I had. We shared the same biological biker father. My biological father was the reason all the motorcycles were there. The bike club gave him a plaque in memory of Brian. Looking back now, I have even more respect for that biker club because they were there for my father with the loss of his son and they were there for me in the loss of my brother. Even to this day I spend time at their clubhouse and they tell me stories of my brother and I growing in the clubhouse from the time we were in diapers and as children.

That day was an emotional rollercoaster and I didn't believe or want to have to think about any of it. The loss of my brother was one of the hardest trials in my life. That day I met new people whom I kept in contact with and built relationships with. After that day, my biological father and I grew closer each year. I would go spend time with him at the clubhouse and I got closer with the bikers. I discovered my roots. People would tell me Brian's story and it was inspiring but it almost made things worse. That story makes me so happy to know that I had a brother that loved me more than anything. He changed his life for me. At the same time it makes me so sad knowing that since Brian, I have never had anyone that loved me that much. I have lost my brother, my best friend, the only man in my life that loved me more than anything. To this day I don't think I will ever get over that. I struggle to believe that I will find anyone who loves me as much as he did. I have had men in my life that loved me but it is not the same love as a big brother has for his little sister.

After time had passed and there was time for healing to set in, my biological father old me the actual story of his death. Brian and my dad had just gotten ice cream and gotten back into my father's work van. When they sat down, two men approached the van. The two men came up Brian's window and asked Brian for his wallet with a gun pointed at his head. My father sat in the drivers seat helpless looking over at his son and fearing for his life. My father couldn't even move to reach his own gun. When Brian told them that he didn't have any money, they pulled the trigger. My father sat in the driver's seat and watched Brian's life get taken away from him. My father's face was covered in the splash of blood from his own son. My father sat there in shock for a moment. As the men ran off, my father took off after them yet did not catch up. To this day he still looks for the men who killed his son and took the life of my brother.

The loss my biological father and I feel surrounding Brian's death is something we hurt together on and we relate with the hurt each year. It never changes. It never gets easier, but at the same time it never gets harder, either. It is just something in life that we have to overcome. I often look back at events in life that happen and wonder how things would have been different if one thing changed. I may have had it rough with my stepfamily and adopted parents, but if I weren't taken away I would have probably been in the van with Brian that day when he was murdered. Who knows what path my life could have taken if just one thing had been changed.

Chapter 5

The Wicked Stepmother

I changed a lot that year. I became bitter towards my parents and blamed them for the time that was lost with my brother. I began to act out and rebel even more and I took a stand for my adopted brother and myself in many ways. My stepmother did not cease in her ways. She tortured my adopted brother, who still wet the bed due to his handicap. He did not have the brain capacity to understand that the way he was being taken care of was not right. She would punish him for being a bed wetter. She took his mattress away and gave him a board and a garbage bag to sleep on each night. She would make him sleep in the same clothes everyday and said it was to teach him a lesson. She said that he would never be allowed to sleep on a mattress ever again if he didn't learn to sleep through the night without wetting the bed. The night came where she told him he was going to sleep in the bathtub because he had wet the bed again the night before. That night as he went to step into the tub, I stopped him and told him to step out of the bathroom. I could not see him suffer like this anymore. My stepmother told him not to listen to me and to do as she said. As my stepmother and I argued back and forth, he ran to his room scared. I put my foot down and let her know that I was not going to let the abuse happen to him anymore. The argument between us got heated. The words were painful on both ends. She turned away from me and walked towards the steps leading up to her bedroom. She went upstairs laughing and she said "just you wait Rach, you won't be going to camp this week." My heart sank for a moment because I was supposed to leave for church camp that weekend and during the argument she had threatened to not let me go if I didn't step away from the bathroom so he could get back in there. I didn't think it was possible for her to stop me from going to camp. I stood my ground to protect him in that situation, and I paid the price for doing so.

As I calmed my brother down and put him back in his own "bed," I heard sirens coming down the street. I opened the blinds, looked out the window and saw two police cars pull into our driveway. Three police officers came through my front door and told me to get against the wall. I was confused as to what was going on. I knew I had not done anything to deserve what appeared to be happening. I told them there was no reason for me to step against the wall. I told them to explain why I had to do so. They turned me backwards, shoved my face into the wall, and put handcuffs on me. They were shouting at me to calm down. At that point I had started to get lippy with them because I knew I was being arrested for no reason. When my stepmother came downstairs and told them that I was threatening her and my brother's life and that they needed to take me away to protect them, I knew exactly what direction she was going with this. I then knew what was about to happen. As I got into the back of the police car I looked back at my home as they drove me to the police station. When I got to the station I kept asking if I could call my adopted father. They would not let me make a phone call. I proceeded to get fingerprinted and the cops did not listen to a word I said. I was a 15-year-old girl that had just been accused of domestic violence. It was perfect timing and she was right, she knew exactly what she was doing when she made that phone call. I really wasn't going to camp. All I could think of in that jail cell was how my life was so close to being ruined by someone and I felt I had no say in anything. I stayed the night in jail until my dad got me out the next day. No one ever believed me about what really happened that night. I ended up on probation and I was given a domestic violence charge on my record. There was nothing I could do to change it. Being in a private school it was very embarrassing for me to get taken out of class weekly by a probation officer. The school did not look to highly upon that situation. They put up with it because my dad paid a lot of money from the subsidy he got monthly from the state for me in order to keep me in that school. That domestic violence charge affects me still to this day. Whenever I get asked whether or not I have been arrested, I have to say yes. It is a situation that didn't make sense and it is hard to explain that to people.

The end of that semester, which was during my sophomore year of high school, my stepmother wanted me out of the house more than ever. She told my dad that she was going to divorce him if he didn't get me out of the house somehow. My dad listened to her and called my adopted mother who at this point had gotten remarried after her affair. They got married when I turned 9 years old. She and her new husband agreed to take me in. I was not fond of the fact that I was going to be living with the mother that was scheming and absent for most of my childhood. I tolerated the visits feeling as though she pitied either us or herself; still not sure which it was, but I had no other choice. At this point it was better than going back into the foster system. I was dropped off an hour north in a new town. I was taken away from my church, away from my private school, away from my soccer team, and away from everything I knew. Everything that had kept me together up until that point was now gone. My stepfather was no better than my stepmother in many ways. I will tell you the reasons why shortly. He and my adopted mother immediately cut off all contact I had with anyone from back home. I didn't have a phone at that time and they didn't let me use the computer so I literally fell off the face of the earth to everyone I had known. I was not allowed to say goodbye to anyone from school or church and I wasn't allowed to explain anything to anyone.

My stepfather would tell my friends from church and school different stories when they would call the house phone. To half of them he told I was pregnant and moved away, the other half he told I had died. He even went through the paperwork in my room and got into my email account I had previously set up. He found the information for my MySpace account, which all of my friends were on, and changed my password so that he was the only one with access to it. He started negative, inappropriate correspondence with friends in my name and started a lot of trouble and caused me a lot of embarrassment. He sent out inappropriate pictures he had taken of me of me to people back at my church. My friends thought it was I who was writing these grotesque things to them. My friends back home had no idea what happened to me. In all the distress I was in, I was thrown into a new city in the middle of nowhere and started up my junior year in a public high school. I was thrown to the wolves alone and broken. My stepbrother, who was a year older than I, was in the same grade as me at this school. I remember him telling me that I was going to get eaten alive at this new school. He said that people would hate me for being a Christian and that the biggest meanest girl in the school named Kenyata was going to tear me apart. I was pretty smart and had learned some street smarts through the years so I took mental notes and I remembered what he said. The first day of school I asked around to people where this girl he spoke of was. When I saw her across the hall I went up to her and told her that I was new and didn't know how to get into my locker and asked her very nicely to come help me. At that moment when she helped me get into my locker, I continued the conversation offered to buy her lunch for helping me and that day I made a new friend. The trials in my life made me very clever. Kenyata and I became inseparable and I will still never forget the look in my stepbrother's eyes when I brought her to the house after school for the first time.

Chapter 6

Final Chances

That year was a challenge. After coming to terms with the loss of my old life and accepting the fact that I would never see or hear from anyone from my past again, I started to learn how to survive in the public school system. After school, I would take the bus to the town I used to live in at my adopted father's house to work at the insurance office that I had maintained throughout all of this where I continued to file papers. The only difference now with maintaining that job was that I had to turn my paychecks over to my adopted mom and stepfather. I was okay with that because even though I didn't see the fruits of my labor, it got me away from my stepfather and stepbrothers. To this day I still have not seen any of that money I worked for that year. They told me that they kept the money because it counted as my rent if I expected to live there with them. The only bonus I saw living with them was that they would at least feed me when I lived with them. One thing I never got at my adopted father's house was a full meal. I still was not happy about living with the mother who abandoned me to live with another man after adopting me. The stepfather had five children. None of his children liked me or accepted me. I was physically and verbally abused by his three boys and by his two daughters on a daily basis. I was outnumbered and I didn't stand a chance in fighting back. My adopted mother saw all of it and never did a thing to stop it. She would bring me into her bedroom and cry to me at night. She would tell me how unhappy she was there with him and that she didn't like how bad my stepdad and the stepchildren treated her. She would tell me that she liked having me around because it took some of the negative attention off her. She asked me to never tell anyone the things that went on because she didn't want me to get taken away from her. I listened to her vent each night because I knew she needed it and I kept my thoughts and feelings on the situation to myself. I took her cries on my shoulder to mean that I meant something to someone. I told myself that the purpose in my suffering there must have been to give her comfort. I was always looking towards a higher purpose. I always knew that there was meaning to my life that was bigger than my present happiness.

I was scared to be alone at home with my stepfather when I came home from school. He was not a good person. He was very prideful, perverted and respect oriented. He would make me do a lot of things I was not comfortable doing. He would have me get dressed up so he could take pictures of me. He would make me get in different poses with different outfits. He would tell me not to tell my adopted mother what he was doing while she was away at work. He would have me put skirts on and walk up the stairs for him and his sons to watch. They would smack my butt and grab my breasts as I dressed up in the scandalous outfits. I went along with it, doing what I thought I could to avoid the anger and tried as best as I could to avoid the physical touching that made me sick to think about.

At the public school I attended, the teachers started to notice that I acted funny at school and my soccer coach mentioned something to the social worker at the school. Eventually, they noticed marks and bruises on me. I avoided telling people at school what was happening because it was embarrassing to admit these things were happening to me. I wanted to have a tough, untouchable image and I had convinced myself that I deserved the things that were happening to me. The school made a call to Child Protective Services. The home visits started. My step dad would not let the social worker into the house when they knocked on the door to talk to him. He would not answer any questions when the school called. The police were at our house many times because of the neighbors calling in on us for domestic disputes. It got to the point where I knew all of their names and was relieved to see them when they came.

They eventually told me that I had to either leave the house as an emancipated minor, since I was 16 at this point, or they would remove me and place me in a foster home. I started moving my belongings out of that house little by little and I got an escape plan together. My boss at the insurance agency would write me two separate checks so that I would give them one and they wouldn't notice much of a difference from what I kept. My stepfather caught on to what I was doing. He went into my bedroom, took the papers and journals I had been writing in, and found out what my plan was. One of the journals was the one I started writing my life story in. I put a lot of time and effort into writing everything down on paper that I went through. I can still remember the feeling of wasted time and pointless existence when he took it all from me and took me out to the backyard and burned it with his lighter right in front of me. The last thing he wanted was for others to hear the story of what happened to me. He told me that no one cared about my story and that I didn't matter. That night after everyone was asleep, I climbed out the second story window, took a backpack of my belongings with me, left everything else behind, and I walked down the street to a house where one of my coworkers lived. I moved out for good and I started living with different families at the insurance office I worked at. Sometimes I would sleep in my friend's van when I didn't have another option. I was very lucky to have that opportunity. The people at the insurance office were all very understanding of my situation and they took turns letting me live with them. I learned a lot from those families. My boss would even let me stay at her house and give me chores to do around her house to make extra money.

Right before my senior year of high school, I begged my adopted dad to let me live at his home again and go back to my private school to be able to graduate from there. My stepmom agreed to let me move back in just as long as I wasn't home in the evenings and as long as I moved out the day I graduated. I started back up my senior year and was able to remedy the rumors my stepdad had spread around about me. I was able to graduate high school with the class I started with. People had actually believed the rumors that I had died. Throughout the year, I lived most weeks with different families at the school so that I avoided problems with my step mom at home. When I did have to stay there I would knock on the window of my adopted brother and he would let me in so I could get to my room to sleep, only to be out of the house in the morning in time to be picked up for school.

Despite all the trials of my last year of high school, I avoided dropping out. I remembered my biological brother Brian and his dedication to pursing his education to make his life right to see me again. Remembering that gave me the motivation I needed to finish. I made it through my senior year. There were so many nights when I would plug my headphones into my disc player and I would blast Simple Plan or Good Charlotte as loud as I could. I would listen to the lyrics and relate to everything they said. At that time, the only people who understood the hurt I was going through was the musicians in the punk rock bands I listened to. Even to this day, if I turn on those songs I used to listen to over and over it brings me back to that place in my life. That isn't exactly the healthiest place to go back to in my mind. Despite that fact, it reminds me how far I have come and it reminds me that the pain I still feel is valid, but the pain inside is not limiting. As I remember the tears I shed listening to those albums, I feel relieved that now I have made it through those painful emotions, which I thought would never go away. Sometimes if I have repressed memories of these past days that I need to write about, I can turn on certain songs and it will bring me right back to those places to be able to put the feelings down on paper. During that time I spent in that house my only escape was my music. The time came when I had to enter into reality and realize that I wasn't safe behind my music and that I needed to stand up again and move forward.

As a child, I was deprived of the little things in life that most people enjoy as a daily norm, such as toothpaste, snacks, shampoo, conditioner and milk. I didn't ever eat any cereal other than off brand rice cereal. God forbid I drank anything other than water at home. I remember thinking that I couldn't wait to be on my own someday so I could go grocery shopping. The first time I was out on my own I went all out. I still do to this day when I go grocery shopping. I buy myself items I never got to enjoy like Fruity Pebbles and chocolate milk. I buy pizza rolls and orange soda. All the things that I had wanted to have back then but never got to enjoy. Everything that I saw all the other kids I went to school with bringing in to lunchtime or seeing these items stocked at their parents houses are the items I stock myself up with. It is almost to the point where I cannot control myself when it comes to buying what I want. Now that I have a job and I can afford to buy these things I don't hesitate to buy myself what I want when I want it. I am just trying to make sure that I don't go too far the opposite way with it.

I have to put a lot of effort into looking normal even today. When people look at me, they see positivity and energy. They feel like I am a role model and they tell me that I have influence. Some people even tell me that they wish they had my life. I just smile and nod when they say these things because they have no idea what goes on beneath the surface. When I look at myself I see a woman who is scared and ashamed yet one who knows how to put on a good show. A normal person can walk by a friend and put their hand on their friend's shoulder as they converse. When I am sitting at my computer at work and someone comes up behind me to tell me something and places their hand innocently on my shoulder, I pull away quickly and I have a million flashbacks going through my mind at that moment. In a split second's time I have to tame those thoughts, pull myself together, look at them as though nothing is wrong, and play it off as though I don't mind that their hand is on my person so that they don't think that I am crazy. I wish that I didn't have to have the fight within myself every time I am innocently touched by someone in my life but I can't help but relate it to the past feelings of being touched when I didn't have a choice in the matter. It isn't my first instinct to willingly tell people that I don't like strangers touching me because when I was a child, my family members sexually abused me. I didn't know when I was a child what was normal and what was to be accepted.

When you are young you don't understand that these things that are happening to you are disgusting and horrible. When your own brothers invite their friends over and they make you take all of your clothes off so they can "play" with you, you think that is normal behavior. When I was 8 years old, my older adopted brother would make me lay me down on the living room floor. He would then let his friends do what they wanted to do with my body. Most often they would place objects inside of me. They said it was a popular game to them to see what could fit into the holes. They would take funnels from the kitchen and pour liquids inside of me to see how much I could hold inside each of my holes. I didn't know what was the right and wrong thing to do in that situation. As I little girl, I was just excited that we had a secret that the parents weren't allowed to know about. When you are little you don't see the effects that you will have later in life when you are old enough to understand what it means that these things happened. At this point in my life, I can see what happened and I can understand now what was going on. At the time it was happening I felt cool and accepted among that group of people. They told me I was just talented at the things I was able to do with my body. As I grew into my teenage years I knew more about what was going on with the added family members that had come into my life. The difference then was that it was embarrassing to admit to people what was going on behind the closed doors. These things went on for years. I had to keep face at church and school and I had to let people think that all was ok. It was embarrassing enough on a lesser level that I didn't have more than one change of clothes and that I didn't even have a lunch to bring into school. The last thing I wanted people to know is that my own family was sexually assaulting me.

After I graduated high school, I left to go on a mission trip to Germany with my church. The ladies at the insurance agency helped me raise money to pay for the mission trips I went on. The mission trip was a great experience and I experienced a different culture and was blessed in so many ways by serving the people in need in that country. It was a beautiful distraction. I was a part of a project that would change people's lives. I was able to talk to young girls overseas that faced the same trials I went through and I had no fear in disclosing my story because I was in a different country and no one that I knew back home could ever find out. We learned about the history of a country other than our own.

In Dresden, Germany I met a guy with dreadlocks who was skateboarding around the town. It seemed as though he was following our church group. I stepped away from the group for a while to talk to this guy and it turns out he was sticking close by us because he heard us speaking English and he wanted to know more about us. I brought him to the group. We ended up taking him back to the missionary house we were staying at and he came to church with us. He then took us all to his school the next day so that we could see what high schools in Germany were like. Through talking to him and getting to know him I found that he had a lot of troubles that most of the United States youth does as well. That gave me perspective and opened my eyes to the fact that there is hurt everywhere. It wasn't just in America and it wasn't just in my home. I still keep in touch with him to this day. I have a gift of meeting great people in life and he was one of the first friends that endured throughout life as a pen pal that kept me in check and provided me hope. That was the year that the World Cup was in Germany so I was in heaven on earth. I played soccer my whole life. I loved soccer and that was the central focus of the town at the time. For that short amount of time in Germany it seemed as though all my problems were gone because I was doing something that gave my life purpose. I only spent 2 weeks there. It had to end at some point and I knew that.

When I came home from Germany, I was dropped back off at my adopted father's house. The church van pulled away and I realized it was time to step back into reality. I walked around to the back door of the where I had always entered into the house. As I walked around the side of the garage, I saw that all of my belongings were in garbage bags and cardboard boxes on the back deck. I went to the neighbor's house to use the phone. I called my dad at work. That was the only place I could ever reach him without my stepmother interfering. I asked him what was going on and why my belongings were on the back deck. He told me there was nothing he could do. He reminded me of how my stepmom only agreed to let me stay there till I graduated and that it was now time for me to move on. There was really nothing I could argue at that point because that was the original deal. I just never believed that she really meant it. When the people in my church found out, the pastor and my youth pastor went to his house to speak with him about the situation. The only thing that was accomplished by them coming over to visit was that my adopted father and stepmother got angry at the church for stepping into their business and they stopped going to church. To this day, they have not gone back to church.

Chapter 7

Homeless and Housing

That was a turning point in my life, I was left with nowhere to go, no place to sleep, no one to call family and no one to turn to. I felt like I used up all of my resources and that my days of asking for help were all used up. I took my things from the back porch. My boss let me keep my stuff in the extra cubicle in the back of the insurance agency. She gave me a key to the office to get in and out for my things. I started finding new friends in the community and I started sleeping on the couch at the office after hours. I would take showers at a local gym that my friend worked at and sometimes I would sleep on the couch in the locker room at the gym. When I stayed at the insurance office I would make sure I woke up early enough to get dressed before the workers came into the office. I didn't want them to know that I had resorted to sleeping on the couch at the office. There were days that I would sleep on back decks of people's homes on porch swings after they had gone to bed. There were also times that I would go to Meijer and sit on the display furniture and act like I was reading something so I could get sleep. As I met new people, I would stay with whoever would have me over for the night as long as they would give me a ride to work in the morning.

My list of friends grew and I came to know many people. I met people in high places and people in low places. I learned a lot about life and I gained a lot of street smarts. Eventually, one of my friends let me borrow his old van in exchange for babysitting his children when I could. I started keeping my clothes in the van and on nights I didn't have a place to go I would just sleep in the van again. I went down many roads at this stage of my life and I experienced a lot about life. I stepped away from church and the friends I had acquired. I was ashamed of where I was at in life and I didn't want anyone to see how low I had gotten.

Surprisingly I stayed away from random sex with the men who helped me out and I didn't get into doing drugs myself. It seemed as though I was surrounded by seedy situations no matter where I went. It was only by God's protection that I stayed a virgin through it all. I had strong morals and that was something that was in my control. Seeing where my mother ended up because of drugs helped make that an easy decision. I definitely did not want to become a prostitute like she was. I had a sense of the value of my own self worth that most girls my age or in my situation didn't have. I was not going to use sex as a tool to get where I needed to be. I believed I was worth more than that and that people should like me and care about me and help me out without that as a playing card. I felt that my own body was the only thing I could finally take control of. I wanted to save myself and the rest of the dignity I had left, for my future husband. I wanted to be able to tell the man that I was going to marry that regardless of all that happened I still did my part to protect myself for him. There were times I assisted in drug sales just to make extra money for gas. Most times I would do the driving for people doing the drug runs since I had a borrowed van. Somehow I maintained purity throughout all of this but I did not hold back on living life on the edge. I would be around people who were doing crazy things in life but I would just watch and learn. The morals I had learned at church kept a guard around my heart and Someone above was definitely looking out for me. I maintained my job at the insurance agency and picked up three other part time jobs to get by. One was at a pizza shop, another was with a catering company and the other was at the ballpark as a waitress. I would work hours on end and some nights I would only get two or three hours of sleep between them all.

I started hanging out with people in Detroit and going to the inner city events such as drag racing by the city airport. I am not referring to the simple show off racing that you see on Woodward. This was real inner city Detroit racing with live guns and cash out and titles thrown down. I was involved in high speed car chases, shootouts and multiple shady situations. My friends had 6-second race cars with parachutes on the back. I lived life on the edge for a while and I am actually quite surprised I made it out untouched. Those groups of people fueled my fire. Living life on the edge was a comfortable place to be for me because it was familiar and fit me. The adrenaline was necessary for me to continue moving. The conventional lifestyle just didn't seem right. Looking back now, having a little more wisdom, I wouldn't go near the same people today that I carelessly associated with back then. I placed myself in situations at that time in my life that I would tell people to do whatever they can to avoid today. I hung around with biker clubs. I made friends with both Harley riders and sport bikers. I made a lot of friends who went off-roading late nights and I had a lot of fun with them at mud bogs and various activities.

I started hanging out with my biological father more and hanging out with the biker club he belonged to. I recognized many of them from my brother's funeral. All the bikers in the club knew who I was. Most of them played a big part in raising me as a baby. My biological father ran the club for a while so he was highly esteemed which made me important to them. The bikers would tell me stories of when I was a baby and share more stories with me about my past and about my brother Brian. I loved the history of the club itself and I was intrigued by the mystique of it all. The clubhouse was a dark and edgy place that the other people in my life suggested that I stay away from. To me the clubhouse was the safest place I could be because I respected them, they knew me and loved me, and I was protected. I was blood to them, which was something I didn't get anywhere else. I felt like I belonged there. That clubhouse felt more like home to me than any of the houses I had stayed in. That to this day is something most people don't understand. People can't understand why I associate myself with my father's biker club or why I put myself in harm's way of the opposing clubs by going down there. They hear stories and watch documentaries about this particular club on Gangland and tell me I am in danger and that I am naïve and living irresponsibly. I personally feel as though I am in more danger away from them. I have been told that if another club found out who I was then I could be placed in an unsafe situation. That makes me more paranoid in everyday situations. Because of who my father is, I always have to be conscious of the people I meet and to whom I say certain things about my life to. Regardless of all of the rumors, negative media coverage and mystique, to me those men in that motorcycle club are my family. They know more about my past than I do. They understand my hurt, they show more concern about me in my life than any of my adopted family ever has. To this day I call that biker club my family. I believe that God has allowed me to enter into that place to be a light in a dark place. I always look at the bigger picture and the unique ways God can use me in life to make a difference in others' lives. The biker club is just an example of a unique opportunity I have to share God's love that most people will never have the chance to do.

Chapter 8

College and Marriage

After several months of running wild and free, I did some soul searching and decided I needed to get my mind back on straight and go off to college. I felt that I needed to get away from the darkness and confusion and try to get right with God again. I went away to the cold state of Wisconsin when I was 17 years old. I started at a small private college to play soccer and study Psychology. I spent a year of my life up there. I got grounded in my faith again and I turned a lot of things that were spiraling downwards in my life around for the better. I worked on learning how to forgive my past abusers and I learned to acknowledge the good parts of my life and the positive people who impacted me throughout the journey rather than dwelling on the bad times. That year I grew a lot as a person and I made a lot of changes to the way I lived life. I learned the faults of the legalism I was raised in, and my eyes were opened to the bigger picture of grace and forgiveness that Christianity offered. I shaped my faith into my own instead of having it as something that was expected of me.

When I came home after that year away, I still didn't have a home or family to come back to. I found rooms to rent on a local website online. I found an excellent set up and rented a room in a mansion with a bunch of people back in my old neighborhood. There were four band members in the house and two waitresses from a local strip club that all lived together. I joined the house with an open mindset. That living situation was not looked upon very highly from people in the church I went to, or even from the people at the college I had come from. I was going into it with a mission's mindset of being able to show non-judgemental love to these people. That was definitely a fun year in my life filled with new experiences. I learned about different ways that people lived life. I gained friends and I learned a sense of community.

I started back up at my jobs that I had left behind and started working at a local bar as well. I maintained the four jobs that year and started going to a local community college. I officially got licensed as an insurance agent and started my career as a young 18-year-old businesswoman. I had a collection of suits I wore on a daily basis that made me feel like I was older than I was. I bought myself a car and I went out and bought a motorcycle and I started over in life. I knew nothing about how to ride a motorcycle, let alone what a clutch was. I had been a passenger on the back for so long that I decided I wanted to be in control of that area of my life as well. I didn't want to feel like I owed someone something when they let me ride with them. I earned those things all by myself. I got help from no one and I was proud of that. I spent that summer building myself up and discovering who I was. Living the life of a girl riding a motorcycle changed everything. I met many people on the road and I discovered many new walks of life. I dated many people that year and learned a lot about life. Most of the men I dated were at least 15 years older than I was. Because of the life I had lived up to that point, I always associated better with older men. I was able to relate more. I was always considered an "old soul." Culturally, it was looked down upon for a younger girl to date an older man but I learned a lot of wisdom from those situations. To me it made more sense than dating a younger man that hadn't experienced anything in life that I had been through because we would not have anything to relate to in life.

I had met a man in his 60's that was a known billionaire. He was very well known in the community. I hung out with him for a while and we would go out to dinner and talk about life. We would go back to his mansion in

Birmingham and he would take me out in his Bentley or Maserati. He took me to the Ferrari dealership twice to help him pick out different cars. I had never seen a briefcase full of money anywhere other than on TV. I remember the day he spent 250 thousand dollars on a Ferrari he drove home as I followed behind him in his Bentley. The catch with him is that he had never been married and he was a very lonely man. He would constantly make me offers that he would buy me my own Ferrari and put me up in a place to live and give me five grand a month if I chose to be his girlfriend. I would entertain his offers and kindly refuse each time he offered. It was tempting. I'm not going to lie. That would be the perfect setup. I could have quit my jobs and I could have retired early. My life would have been set! I would have had no reason to write this book because my life would have seemed perfect. I can't say that I didn't consider his offer, because I did run it through my mind, but at the end of the day I had to remind myself that no amount of money could buy your dignity. I enjoyed spending time with him, but I didn't love him. I could not justify being a gold digger. If I had agreed to his proposals I would have fit the title well. I still to this day keep in touch with him and we are still good friends. He tells me stories of throughout the years the different girls who took him up on his offers from time to time. He has a respect for me now that I have my career and he watched me struggle through it when he had offered to make life so simple for me. He still tells me that it was my choice to continue on struggling throughout it all because his option would have allowed me to live an easier life. I still hold to my morals though and I am thankful that I maintained my dignity through it and learned the life lessons that came my way.

That summer back from my freshman year at college I met a guy near my home town who was also a Christian. He shared the same beliefs on life as I held dear. He was younger than any of the other guys that I dated so it was new and out of my comfort zone. For some reason, it seemed right. He rode a motorcycle as well and he had a great family. I was seeking someone with a nice family that I could be a part of. That was a huge factor in my dating endeavors. We seemed to have the same basic ideas on what we wanted out of life. We hung out everyday and we got close very fast. We both had the intent to wait until marriage to have sex or any form of intimacy. We spent almost every day together. We would ride our motorcycles together everywhere and stay up till three am hanging out and then go to work at 8 am the next morning exhausted but smiling. Our relationship reached a point four months in where we reached a level of sexual intimacy. We both caved into a feeling of lust that we both spent our lives trying to resist. The passion was heavy and the fulfillment made the wait seem a pointless waste of so much pleasure in life. We continued to make love in secret and hide our physical affections from family and friends in our inner Christian circle. There was a point in time where things got awkward. Guilt began to creep in. The sexual intimacy that was once so fulfilling now felt so empty and full of shame. I had spent my whole life saving this for my husband. In my mind, this must have meant that now he had to be my husband. We both realized that we had broken vows to ourselves. I remember the discussion we had when we both shared our guilt of not saving ourselves sexually for the one we were going to marry. We both agreed that the only way to fix this problem was to get married. The same legalistic rules that we were taught all along shaped our guilt-led decision to get married just because we had sex. When I mentor women now, I make sure they understand that getting married based on those reasons will only end in heartbreak. It seemed crazy and everyone around us wondered why we were moving so fast in our relationship. We would tell people that we were so in love that we just couldn't see life apart from each other. I'm pretty sure we even justified it to ourselves that we actually thought we were blissfully in love. In our culture of the legalistic Christians, it would have been highly looked down upon if people actually knew that we were sexually intimate. We held onto that secret and until this book is published his family and our friends will still have believed that we got married for love.

We were married within 6 months of meeting each other. Needless to say, I did not go back away to college but rather settled down in a place with my new husband. I changed my career and started nursing school a year after we were married. We struggled each day to try to love each other and to make things work. We continued to believe that love was a choice and as long as we kept choosing to love each other every new day then we would be just fine. At first it was easy to do because the marriage feeling was new. We had been distracted the past couple months with wedding planning and honeymoon planning. Those are fun things that can make anyone happy for a time. Marriage was a new experience and the beginning is full of the fun parts. We set up a home and bought furniture and decorated our new place. We set up our wedding gifts and played into the idea of a marriage with hope. In this marriage I learned what it was like to finally have a source of stability and I finally knew what it was like to have a real family around me for the first time.

I felt a sense of safety and comfort in that new situation. I finally had someone who promised to always love me and told me he would never abandon me like the other people in my life had. Even his family took me on as their own. They all invested in me, they acted as a real family, and showed me love I had never experienced. They promised to love me and be there for me no matter what. They would ask how my day at college was or call to see how work was going or call to just talk or ask us to go to dinner. This was a way of life I had never experienced. Never before had anyone cared how I scored on an exam or how my new classes were going. This was a life of normalcy. It was nice. That was the only true sense of family I had ever experienced. I finished nursing school and became a registered nurse. While I was in nursing school the relationship with my husband ended up not being the greatest. I am sure that you are very surprised! We began to get to know each other through this struggle of finding love in each other. We realized very quickly that we were not compatible for each other. Our struggle now fell back onto the legalistic view that bonded us into this guilt bound relationship in the first place. Neither of our beliefs would accept divorce as an option. We stuck it out and were both living miserable lives. Luckily in our predicament one thing we had in our favor was that we did not have any children. The fact that we didn't have any kids at that point without me using birth control just goes to show you one of the issues we had in our marriage. I felt more alone in that marriage than I had felt during the time when I was out living on the streets. At least at that point in my life I had men who were actively interested and trying to be intimate with me. It was nice to know that I still had someone who was going to be there whether they wanted to or not. Selfishly, the fact that I had a family that still loved me was all that mattered. The family had no idea the problems we were facing, they all looked at us as the trophy couple that had everything right.

As the months went on, our relationship became futile. There was so much hurt and I spent so many nights crying myself to sleep. He told me many times he was just not attracted to me anymore and that he was interested in other women but just not me. I would lie in bed at night tossing and turning. To the left of me was a man that I called my husband - a man that was supposed to be my own. This was the man who was supposed to give me more love than I ever imagined and he was supposed to be the one that made it possible for me to finally sleep through the night safely. I can't say that I have ever felt as alone as I did while I laid next to him at night. There was such a great divide between us. He was physically within reach yet our hearts were so far apart. There was a presence of separation, guilt and regret. There were nights I would roll over to hug him and I would get pushed back to my side of the bed and he would tell me to let him sleep and to stay on my side of the bed. There were nights that my past flashed back in front of me and I needed to be held and to feel like I was loved but I was fearful of turning towards my husband in fear of further rejection. I felt so hopeless and so alone lying there in the bed next to him. Most nights I slept on the couch or in the spare bedroom just to avoid the emptiness of having a void return of my affections.

There were nights where I would get up in the middle of the night and go into the kitchen where I kept my medications that were prescribed to me for depression and anxiety. I would take a handful of Xanax or a bunch of pain-killers just to numb the emotional pain in hopes of falling asleep to forget the pain I was in. It was an attempt to make reality stop and to take the self-defeating thoughts away. It got to the point where my husband would hear me going through the pill bottles and would actually get out of bed and get to me in the kitchen before I would be able to take the pills and he would take them from me and hide them. He didn't stay to comfort me in those moments. He would just tell me that I was crazy and needed help to get over my issues. He said that it would look bad on him if I went crazy and killed myself. I would lean against the kitchen wall and slowly slide down till I hit the floor. Those nights my tears seemed to be unending. So many nights I spent alone and wondered how I let myself fall to that level and end up in a relationship where I felt more alone than in the days that I didn't even have a roof over my head. I was stronger than this, wasn't I? I felt more wanted when I was being sexually abused because at least those people in my life wanted me physically. It got to the point where I missed that. I missed being wanted sexually. I missed being found attractive.

There was emotional verbal and physical abuse throughout the relationship. I tolerated it and just thought to myself "It's ok. I've been through worse." I turned the other cheek and justified it by telling myself the cliché phrases and convincing myself that I deserved it for having so many psychological issues he had to deal with during my depressive moments. He would play out situations I had told him about that I went through with my stepfather in the past and when we got into fights he would put me through them again. He would corner me in the bathroom like my stepfather would and yell right into my face to the point where I couldn't breathe. That would put me into flashback mode. It was not a healthy situation. There were moments in those episodes that I was afraid of how toxically I would react to him on those situations if they continued to happen. I had grown up learning to protect myself in whatever way necessary. I can remember my anger in the outbursts against the men who hurt me in the past and the level of rage could have easily been fatal. That was the last thing I wanted to let myself get to the point of. I had tried everything to make him love me and become attracted to me again. I lost weight. I changed my hair. I bought new clothes. I tried everything I could do to present myself to him so that he would fall for me again. I have to admit in regret and shame, that I even tried bringing my best girlfriend into the picture to see if he was into men rather than women and I wanted to rule that out. Let's just say that my friend was a trooper and it was evident that my husband was very into women It was clear that the problem was indeed me. Our struggles continued with no improvement and we just lived our separate lives in the same household and had no physical or sexual contact. I had even stopped forcing him to give me a hug when he came home from work. It was so hard to hug someone who wouldn't even move or lift his arms to embrace me back. I felt like I was hugging a stand up doll to make myself happy.

There was a point in time when another girl came into the picture. This girl had been his high school sweetheart. She was the one that my mother in law warned me about. She told me about his history with her, that she was always his kryptonite and they were inseparable. I didn't take her advice. I decided to trust my husband. He wanted to hang out with her and have her over all the time when she moved back into town. The ironic part is that I was the one who picked her up and drove her home from Tennessee when my husband told me that his friend needed help getting herself and her son back to Michigan. That is one trip I regret taking.

After I brought her home I helped her get settled in to a local apartment. There were nights I would come home from work at three in the morning and they would be hanging out in the garage drinking beers and listening to music. In my mind I thought that maybe if he noticed that I was trusting him and giving him freedom to hang out with his old best friend who had moved back to town he would appreciate it and love me more. I was wrong. Our relationship grew more and more distant each day. She had introduced him to marijuana. They obtained medical marijuana cards together and he became a bigger pothead than I have ever met in my life. Now don't get me wrong I have nothing against people who smoke marijuana. There are many people who benefit from it medically and I support that. In this situation as a nurse it would have been detrimental to my career to have a positive drug screen just because I breathed in the air around them. I was surrounded by smoke all the time and my career was now at risk. The two of them were ambivalent and they would have friends over and sell and smoke weed daily. It was turning into a scenario where I needed to be away from my own house in order to avoid having cannabis in my urine sample during my work physicals. Watching their relationship grow hurt so deep. The more I tried to step in and ask him to back away the more resistance he put towards me and it only made things worse. The time came when he didn't come home one night after having dinner with her and I was immediately struck down and placed in panic mode. The moment had come when my fear was evident. I sent each of them a message asking where he was and I sent them at the same time. I asked him where he was and I asked her what time he left the night before. The text messages crossed at some point and she responded to my text with one she meant to send to him. The text read "So are we going to keep moving forward with this or are we going to have to take a break?" I sent her a text back saying "Are you sure that was meant for me?" I haven't heard from her since that day. From that day forward I made it clear that she was never allowed near our house again. I read through my husband's phone when he came home and went to bed. I read the texts he sent her telling her that he regrets getting married to anyone other than her and wondered what would have been different if she never moved away. He told her that marrying me was the worst mistake he made in his life and the texts went back and forth. Eventually I told him that I had looked through his phone at the messages at night and I asked him to lock his phone so that I wouldn't be tempted to read them. I stuck with the marriage for another year and tried to forgive but through all that eventually I became strong enough to realize that I had married someone that hit too close to my past.

My friends all told me that I was crazy for giving him another chance and that I had no reason to stay married to him. They had all encouraged me to leave him from early on in the decline of the relationship when I started telling them about our problems. I hesitated for a long time, not telling anyone what went on because he told me that I wasn't allowed to talk about the things that went on since he was my husband and that he got to choose what people knew about our relationship.

There was one occasion where we were in a fight and it got so escalated that he told me he wanted nothing to do with me. He threw me out the front door and locked it behind me. I was left out there barefoot in my pajamas. It was almost midnight and I had to work the next day. I was very shaken up because of the yelling that had just taken place. I picked myself up of the ground in front of my condo and I looked around to see if anyone just saw what happened. I didn't even have my cell phone with me. It was too late to wake any of the neighbors. I pounded on the door begging him to let me in. I sat out there in the cold for about 20 minutes until I realized that unless I did something I would not make it to work in the morning and my life would begin to fall apart. I knew that I had brought myself too far to just give up and let my life fall apart like this again. At that moment I then saw that I was losing control of my life and I couldn't be a victim any longer. I went around to one of the bedroom windows. I broke the screen off and broke the window open to crawl back into the house. I got my phone and I locked the bedroom door. I called my friend Holly and told her I needed help. She was at a party with friends at the time, and she had been drinking. She told me to hold tight till she called another girlfriend that was at a local hospital 15 minutes away where our friend was having a baby. Holly sent one of our girlfriends that was at the hospital to come get me so that she could stay on the phone with me. I picked up my bottle of Xanax and I told Holly that I needed to take them because my heart was beating so fast that I felt like I would die from a heart attack if I didn't calm down. I was in a sheer panic state. My husband was beating on the bedroom door telling me that if I didn't open the door he would break it down. I poured the last five pills into my hand and put them into my mouth. As I swallowed the pills, the door cracked down the middle and the bedroom door broke open. My husband came through the door and grabbed me and pinned me to the floor. The next few minutes were a blur as I tried to picture myself being somewhere else knowing that the torment he was putting me through was about to fade with the help of the Xanax that would start kicking in shortly and I knew that I had help on the way. I laid there helpless and listened to the shouts and tried to hold my breath and keep my mind out of the situation to avoid letting the harmful words sink in and take me to a darker place. As he picked me up from the ground, he shook me and threw me into the wall. He came back over and grabbed my wrist. I heard banging on the front door. I got away from his grip and ran to the front door. I unlocked it and Charis came inside to help me. She handled my husband as I grabbed my cell phone and work scrubs and ran out the door. I remember him yelling at us as we ran towards her car that I am never allowed back in the house again and we better hope that we never see him again. Charis took me to the hospital where our friend was delivering her baby. I remember being in a fog and a daze as the medications kicked in. I couldn't even tell you where I slept that night because I was so out of it. The night I just shared with you was just one example. Those are the typical fights that would go on between my husband and I behind closed doors. My friends heard all these stories and that's why they would tell me that I was crazy for putting up with it. I would remind them every time that I was okay with it because I had experienced worse and that I would never be able to find anyone else that would love me. That concept is hard for people to understand, but for me it just made sense.

Eventually it had gotten to the point where my own friends wouldn't listen to my complaints about my marriage any more because I didn't take any of their advice on the matter. I was mad at them at the time but I have come to learn the reasons why they had to show tough love and I now advise people in the same way with an added resume of experience. If there are problems in your life and you acknowledge them but refuse to change them then you have no right to complain about them. The marriage ended after four and a half years of continuous struggles. I walked away from everything that we had built up together. His family instantly disowned me without asking any questions about my side of the story. To them it seemed like I was the bad guy in the situation. They had no idea that we were failing at our picture perfect marriage. They had no idea of his new drug habits or his new personal affairs. It was as though it was all a show. He would not admit it to anyone who brought it up. He would just tell them I was crazy and that I wanted attention. People would never believe that he would do such things. To be honest, it really was a production. It was a show and I was the producer. I was moving forward in a screenplay where the demise was impending. I realized through that experience, that his family was never truly my own family. The emotions of being without a true family and the emotions of my continual abandonment that I thought ended at marriage, continued on as my husband had just given up on me. I had no choice left but to move on. There was no time to look back. There was no time to stop in place and deal with things. If I didn't continue to move forward, I would just sink downwards into the quicksand of life that was always trying to bring me under. Despite the challenges, I was resilient. I kept moving forward with my head held high like nothing was wrong. Sometimes the love you feel at the time is not worth the pain you sustain when it is gone.

Chapter 9

American Dream Shattered

As I sat down at a small town coffee shop to begin to write this book, I sat between two men in their late 70's. These men were curious about what I was doing with a laptop at a bar stool of their diner when they have never saw me there before. I explained to them my love for small town cafes due to the appeal of a quiet place to be where life seemed much simpler to me. The men tried to hide the fact that they were glancing over at my screen to see what I was writing. One asked if he could read it and the other asked what my purpose for writing was. I shared a general summary of my intentions and goals and they both were very supportive in letting me get back to it because they hoped to get the first copy. I will never forget the man to my right in a corduroy jacket and a baseball cap. The man leaned over to me and said in a still small voice "this chapter of your life that you are in right now, make sure that you are the one who writes that chapter." I remember dwelling on what he said. I had told them about my current marriage situation at the time and how I was fighting against the divorce that seemed inevitable. In retrospect this man was very wise. In other chapters in this book I was a child and didn't have a say at how the chapters were written. At that time I could only participate in how to live through them and keep moving forward. My divorce was something I could actually take control of. Control was the one thing I never had. Even though this was something that I never saw coming while going into it, a divorce was something I never wanted to be a part of my book. My story was supposed to have a happily ever after ending. A divorce was a process I thought I could never gain the strength to begin, but it was something that deep within I knew had to be done. Otherwise my whole story would end with me as a failure who had not learned from the past and my life would have been wasted.

The day finally came when we stopped ignoring the process that was unfolding. My husband and I decided we were going to get this process over with and file the divorce papers without a lawyer. We were both in agreement that it needed to happen and that we needed to stop delaying the inevitable. He had told me he would walk with me through it and that he would support me and be cooperative in the filing process. I believed him. I filed the first set of papers. From that day forward the whole process took only two months. It turned out that I was the one who had to research the laws of divorce, get the paperwork together and make the process happen because he wanted to take no part in the responsibility of filing. He told me that helping me would make him look bad. During those two months we tried to negotiate how we were going to handle things and how we were supposed to notify the family of our decision. He decided that we were not going to tell any of the family until it was finalized. I stuck to that deal and I did not tell the family or give any reasons of why it had to happen. During this time my husband had been notifying his family of the process and of what was going on behind my back. I continued on with the divorce process not knowing that his family was hearing what he was telling them from his side of the story. They sat back and watched the process take place.

When the time came for the divorce to be announced and to come out in the open, I could not contact his family or even step foot on their property. From what he had told them, his family saw it from the glasses he put on for them, and immediately cut me off from their lives. I had no communication and no closure at all. My husband told me that if I contacted his family or went to their homes he would call the police and have me arrested for whatever he would make up for them to do so. I had seen this happen before in life with my stepmother and I was not about to let that happen in my life again. It wasn't worth it. I was devastated. The family was closed off to the details and had no idea about who this man really was behind closed doors. They didn't know about the drugs, alcohol and girl he fell in love with on the side. They had no idea about the affair or about the abuse that went on within our marriage. All they saw was the process unfolding and it appeared as though I was hiding it. It appeared as though I had timed it and planned everything out to benefit my timeline for my life with my new nursing career. Really when you take a step back, I was hiding it. I was hiding the process because that is what my husband had asked me to do at the time. So I get it. It was deceitful, though it was not in my character to do so, and it did look bad on my part because I had just gotten settled into my new career as a nurse. Given the situation, it did look bad from an outsider's perspective. They did not even question the motives around it to find out more. That was really not their business either, and to avoid hurt and further torture it was just best for me to move forward without closure.

From that time forward I had signed everything over to my husband. I found a car to lease and a house to rent and I walked away from the marriage with my furniture and clothing. I left the house while he was away on vacation to avoid a messy ending. From that day forward I began a new life in a new city. I made sure to keep my address a secret to avoid further conflict. I walked away from all the mutual friends, the town, the memories and the family. I had faced the fact that once again, I was on my own. It was a good reminder that the only person in life that I could count on to take care of me was myself. The only constants in my life were my job and the church I had gotten involved in since the affair had broken into our marriage the year prior. My life went from knowing exactly how it was going to be and the direction I was headed, to all of a sudden having no direction, no new goals and searching for what my purpose in life was.

I thought I had everything set. I was going to have my husband, a home we built together, and a career at the local hospital where I could put down roots and move up the clinical ladder. When the marriage fell apart, it left me wondering where home base was at that point. Was I supposed to put down new roots in the same place I started or should I start digging again somewhere else? What was even keeping me at the job I had started? Once again, everything was in question. This seemed to be a process I kept getting into. It seemed like this was becoming my new profession in life. I started over new once again. I was at a new job, a new church and a new county. I leased a new car, moved into a new home and made new friends. Again I became a new person and took the wisdom gained through it all with me. Once again I had to put on a smile, move forward, and chalk it up to experience. I will go into more detail later in the book but the key point is that I didn't stop or turn around. In the moment of defeat I had to move forward and forget about the pain.

Chapter 10

Bitterness about remarriage

After my divorce, the question I was faced with most was "do you think you could ever get married again?" I tossed that question around many times. At first, after my divorce, I hated men and the idea of dating. I thought that nothing good could ever come out of a marriage. I was deeply hurt after my divorce and I never wanted to feel that kind of pain again. I remember the days of being single before I got married, and I remember that I had more happiness then. I was not happy during my marriage. That feeling made me believe that I would never want to get married again because happiness must only be available if I am single. I had to realize that that feeling I was harboring was bitterness. I felt bitterness towards my husband. I felt bitterness towards his family. I was also harboring bitterness towards my family for choosing his side. Bitterness is not something that anyone should harbor in his or her heart. It will tear you apart and it will leave you empty and unwilling to be refilled.

As time went on, I realize that all I wanted from the beginning was a husband. I wanted someone to love and to take care of. I wanted a companion. In my marriage I had that at first and it seemed like it was what I wanted. Through the struggling during the marriage and throughout the divorce process, I realized that it wasn't marriage that was a bad thing, but that I had just married the wrong person.

It was then that I realized that marriage itself was not a bad thing. The mistake with my marriage was marrying the wrong person. I learned from my divorce that it was not a good idea to marry someone after only knowing him for a matter of a few months. I learned my lesson there, and that is something I will never do again. I have had friends come after me and do the same thing. I offer my advice to them, and I tell them that it is impossible to know someone well enough in just a few months to make a proper decision on marriage. Giving advice seems to be pointless sometimes. A feeling that you are "in love" blinds people. Whether you have been through an experience or not, most people will not listen to your advice. People have to learn by going through the experience themselves. It is sad that is how it works because people can save a lot of trouble by just listening to advice. It always ends up with someone saying "I told you so."

I gained wisdom through my experience, and I gained a sense of knowing exactly what I'm looking for now. I want to be married again more than anything. I do realize that it will take time. It can not be rushed. In my life I have never had a stable family or stable person to love me so for me a marriage is more deeply desired. What I desire out of the marriage is someone that will love me, be there for me and not abandon me. The love should go both ways. That is what most people strive for. That is what most people want in a marriage. When it comes down to it, companionship is the purpose of dating. People want a companion. I want a life companion, and I want someone I can love. So the answer to the question "do you think you will ever get married again" is yes. It wasn't the marriage that was a bad thing - it was the combination of people that was a bad thing. Marriage is a good thing, and it has a lot of benefits. Divorce happens frequently. The divorce rate is greater than 50%. This is a statistic that I never wanted to be a part of. I have to suck it up and realize that now I am part of that statistic. That does not mean that marriage is out of the question for me. It just means I have to be wiser the next time around. Love takes time and it is something I am working towards and striving towards. I believe that God has the perfect man planned for me and he will come into my life when I least expect him to.

The question for me is not whether I will get married again, but the question is whether or not I will love again. Love is something that is hard to do in the first place. With all the trauma and abandonment that I've gone through it makes it harder to trust or love. In order to truly love, you have to trust. So that is my goal. My goal will not be to get married. My goal will first be to love. Once I can learn to love again I can then approach the idea of marriage. So it is not out of the question. It is a common theme to be bitter and hate the opposite sex after going through a divorce, or any breakup for that matter. The key here is time. Time can heal and time does heal. First you have to learn to forgive yourself and move forward and realize that next time it won't look the same as the first time. Nothing will ever be the same as it once was. Things in your life will look different. Change is not bad, just different. Each situation and each person is different.

To anyone that feels the bitterness currently, and is opposed to getting married ever again, I can encourage you to just wait, have patience and just give it time. You need time to heal. During that healing time it is easy harbor bitterness. It is part of the process, but it doesn't have to be an end result. In time you can love, forgive, learn, and trust.

Another key part of the divorce vs. remarriage debate is admitting your mistakes in the marriage. Marriage takes two people. To file for divorce only requires one person but needs to end with two people in agreement to do so. Admitting your fault in the marriage allows you to learn how you can change to be a better person in the long run. To say that I didn't make any mistakes in my marriage would be a lie. I have learned a lot through the process and I have learned a lot about myself post-divorce. I have learned a lot about the things I need to change and the things I need to work on. I have also realized the things I still need help with.

There are a lot of things in my own life that I struggle with. There are scars from my past that I brought into my marriage. That was not fair for my husband to have to take on. Anytime you go through traumatic events, you are going to change as a person. That is a valid fact that can't be argued. Your circumstances affect you but they don't have to define you. You can't change what has happened to you, but you can change how you react to it. When you choose to marry someone you choose to take on their struggles and their burdens. You take two lives and you intertwine them into one. Each person has his own story. Each person has their own battles they face, and each has their scars.

Marriage is a matter of taking on the hurt, sharing the hurt and helping each other along the way. Having a companion is a healthy thing, it is a good thing and marriage is a beautiful thing. I will get back there someday, but first I realize I need to heal myself before I bring my burdens on to someone else without first putting the work in myself.

Chapter 11

Bicycle Accident

After the divorce, three months had past where I couldn't go back to write any more of this book. Each time I tried to write, I couldn't put myself in a place where I had to write about my divorce and admit the hurt and struggles the divorce process put me through. In those initial weeks after the divorce, I secluded myself at home. I was hurting on a deeper level than I thought I would be. I did not see an end in sight. I would sit on the couch in the new house I had just rented and spend hours in the recliner with a blanket and a cup of tea just staring out the window. I would watch families outside playing in the street and I watched people jog by on the sidewalk with their dogs. I saw people pedaling by on their bicycles and I heard people ride by on their motorcycles. It reminded me of the biker lifestyle I used to be a part of that gave me joy in life. I questioned everything about my life during that time. I wondered what the purpose or meaning was to begin with if it was only going to fall apart the way it did. I wondered if I had screwed up to the point of no return. I stared at my phone waiting for a call or text of encouragement that never showed up. I had come to realize that those encouraging calls didn't show up because I had kept my word to my husband about keeping the divorce a secret until it finalized. I listened to him when he told me not to tell anyone and I isolated myself through it all. That is something I learned never to do again. I learned through that situation that it is important to always have a support system in sight. I had already sunk into a deep depression at that point. I was only 23 years old and I was already divorced. I even began to question whether I even had a purpose in life anymore. The negative thoughts spiraled downward. I reminded myself of how my own biological family didn't even want me in the beginning. I then reminded myself about how my adopted family gave me up. Now my married family whom I thought would break this cycle disowned me. What good did I have to offer to anyone? I truly believed at that time that the common denominator must have been me. Those were the thoughts going through my mind. For a brief time the suicidal thoughts came back to my mind and I wanted this pain to just end.

This feeling of loneliness I hid inside was so deep that it consumed me. I would tell my friends at work how alone I felt and that I was scared of who I would have to support me if anything bad ever happened to me. I had lost my adopted family, my husband and his family that had promised to become my family forever. My biggest fear was to get in a tragic accident and have no one to take care of me if I ever ended up paralyzed or if something worse happened. I truly believed I had no one left at all. The friends around me had their own lives and struggles of their own. It was a scary state of mind being scared and living in a new house all alone when I have never lived alone in my life. Even when the situations were unsafe or if I was with strangers, I always had someone nearby. I obtained my concealed pistol license and bought a gun to protect myself. Having a pistol in the house made me feel safer to an extent. Finally I cried out for help. I decided it was time to let the people in my church know what was going on with me. I knew I needed support and that I needed prayer for strength most of all. Even though I felt distant from them I knew that I needed them at that time. Letting them in was the best decision I made in that period of my life. The friends at church became my backbone and kept me standing. They reminded me that God loved me even through the struggles.

After I reached out for help, I gained some new energy. The fear I had held inside of being alone in personal tragedy was put to the test one day. Before I went to work that day I had decided that it was time to get off the couch and stop crying about my current depression I had fallen back into and that I was going to be active. I had gotten myself into a sad state of physical nature. I had allowed myself to gain 30 pounds in two months' time. I had began to binge eat. Through all of that I had brought myself to the point of acquiring an eating disorder on top of all of this. I would eat constantly and I didn't care. I would eat to the point of making myself sick to where I couldn't get up because of the abdominal pain that the binging caused me. I got to the point where my hospital scrubs wouldn't even fit me anymore. So that day I got off the couch and went for a ride around the block on my bicycle. What I thought was going to be an uplifting workout turned into a trial and test I never expected.

From fleeting memories surrounding the accident, I truly have no recollection of what happened that brought me to that point on that day. I remember waking up on a backboard c-collared in the back of an ambulance. As I lifted my hand to my head to see what hurt so bad I felt my skull shift in two pieces and felt soft tissue beneath. As a nurse, my next assessment was to check if there was bleeding from the ear. As I moved my hand down my skull and removed my finger from my ear to see blood and clear fluid flowing out, I knew from my medical background that was a fatal sign. The paramedic placed a non-re-breather mask over my face and said "stay with us. We aren't going to lose you now." I remember looking up as I heard the sirens and feeling as though I was fading away and falling down a ravine. As I drifted off I knew at that moment I was either slipping into a coma due to the brain injury or I was dying due to the intracranial pressure buildup and bleeding out. I remember praying desperately at that moment that God would give me a second chance and keep me alive and I asked him to forgive me for wasting my life by sitting on the couch and feeling depressed. I promised that I would write my book and tell my story. It was in that moment I knew my life was worth so much more than what I allowed myself to give credit for. In that moment all color surrounding me turned white. I slipped back into unconsciousness not knowing what the outcome would be. The ambulance was on their lunch break and had driven down the side street I was riding my bicycle on. They just happened to be on scene the moment I hit the sidewalk. Talk about miracles! I found that out after looking up my medical records from that day. Minutes later I woke up in the resuscitation room of the local trauma center. Trauma surgeons, neurologists, doctors, nurses and medical residents surrounded me. That moment when I looked up and regardless of the pain I was in I knew that I was alive. That was the moment I knew that I was alive for a purpose. I knew that everything was going to be ok even if I ended up paralyzed.

I remember a doctor asking me if I had family they could call to notify. In that moment when I said "no," I was not depressed like I thought I would be when I had to make that statement. At the time it didn't matter that I didn't have family or a support system. All that mattered was the fact that I was alive. I had a peace in that situation that I didn't think was possible. From the time I got my CT scans and tests done to the time they brought me to a procedure room to get my head stapled, the last contact in my phone was contacted. That person responded to the phone call and came up to the hospital just in time to hold my hand while they put the staples in my head. They put them in without using numbing medication and without cleaning the site first. I am a major germ phobic so that really bothered me. I have never experienced pain like that before. Having staples go into my scalp was terrible pain! The person who arrived first contacted others in my phone for me. The tests revealed that I had a temporal bone fracture lying over the carotid artery. I had a traumatic brain injury, a broken jaw, pneumocephalus (pocket of air in the brain from a skull fracture), hemotympany (blood filled ear canal), loss of hearing, loss of sensation and loss of function on the right side of my face, and benign positional vertigo (dizziness and nausea with any movement of the head). The doctors said that I was lucky to even be alive. They said I was very close to bleeding out and dying. They said that if the ambulance that happened to be driving by on their way to lunch hadn't stopped at the moment of impact that they witnessed as I fell, I would not have gotten transported to the trauma center fast enough. Luckily, the trauma center was only a mile away. I would not have survived the accident that day if it were not for the circumstances lining up in my favor that day. That was a completely planned out situation that I believe God allowed to be set up just as it was. I don't believe in coincidence. I believe that everything happens exactly when it is supposed to. That accident was necessary in my life.

By the time I got to my room on the neurology unit of the hospital, there were at least 10 people in my room. Some of the people I recognized. Some were people from church that I had not met before. These people surrounded my bed and began to pray over me for healing. There were flowers and bears on my bedside table and my room was lit up with love. The friend who came first had contacted these people who showed up to support me. Those people then called others to come visit. My room was filled with people that I didn't even know coming in and out of the room all evening. People cared about me enough to come pray for me. I believe those prayers helped me heal quickly. The first few days after I got home from the hospital were rough. I needed help eating and getting to the bathroom. I needed help standing and even getting dressed. I can still remember being spoon fed the best tomato soup I ever had. From the day of the accident and a week later, I was not left alone for a minute. These people had made a sign up sheet and people took turns staying with me, caring for me, mashing potatoes for me and making sure I was ok throughout the night. After all the prayers I was back to 80% functioning 10 days later. When I went back to the ER to get my staples out, they were amazed at how well I was doing. They were surprised that I had such impressive cognitive and motor functioning 10 days after the accident. I told them that I had to be strong because I was taking care of myself and I had to push through to get back to work to support myself. I was determined to get better. I told them that my God works miracles and that I was living proof of a Higher Power that some people question. I went back to work two weeks later. My work was very flexible with me. They put me at the triage desk the first couple weeks back so that I didn't have to do heavy labor that would put excess pressure on my brain.

Through the support and prayers I was able to regain most of my functioning. To this day I still have deficits and problems with speech and memory at times, but I am learning to live with the deficits. That support group that was brought into my life at that time has stayed faithful and is part of my support group even to this day. It was in that situation that I learned that family does not mean blood. I learned that day that I am not alone. My biggest fear in the divorce and my struggle of loneliness was thrown right at me as I faced my first real near death experience. It was through that traumatic event that I finally learned that God was looking out for me. He was never going to leave me alone. That is the time that I was finally at peace with the divorce even though I felt as though my life had been falling apart. That accident showed me new life and new hope. It sparked my flame inside for utilizing my purpose and for seeking out my unique ability. The time I spent wasting my life and crying about my past was over.

On a recent flight, I sat next to a Neurophysisict who works at Harvard University. We had a discussion about traumatic brain injuries and neuropsychological disorders. He told me about the research he was doing concerning these topics. He showed me presentations he put together and showed me results of some of the studies he was in the process of doing. I told him about my accident. I showed him my scans and the results that I had stored in my phone. After reviewing my case, the physicist was in shock. He did not believe that the case I showed him was my own. He told me that the level of functioning that I was at (8 months after the accident at that point) was unheard of. He said that it does not make sense scientifically or medically. I was very confident in my response by telling him that I believed in miracles and that I believe that when the people from my church came to pray healing over me after the accident, it changed my outcome. To this day I still believe that and the more I tell my story of the accident alone people have been touched by my story and it makes it worth going through.

Chapter 12

Little Conveniences

Given everything I had been through and the recent divorce, who would have thought that filling out paperwork at your doctor's office could be so emotional? The lady at the counter asked me if I had any status changes the past year. I laughed and said "yes." She handed me a clipboard and told me to update my information. When I sat in the lobby to fill out paperwork, I came to the line that asked for my emergency contact. For a second I froze and a thousand thoughts, images and fears flew through my mind. I began to breathe faster until I stopped breathing. I held my breath in a panic state. Choosing a new emergency contact was a decision I thought I would never have to make again. I can still remember in college and during high school not knowing what name to write down because my family was not reliable as an emergency contact. At that time I was naïve to an extent so I was perfectly comfortable putting a friends name down. When I got married at 19 and I went to all my doctors appointments I felt content and comfortable for the first time putting down my husband's name. I felt like I finally had someone that I could trust to take care of me. I never thought I would have to put another thought into it again.

When I thought about whom I would put down at this stage in my life I struggled. My family was out of the question, my husband was gone, and I realized at this stage in my life that friends come and go and the circle will always be changing. It is a scary thought to have to worry about who is going to be contacted in an emergency situation. The person you choose to fill that role should know you better than anyone else. That person needs to know your end of life wishes. That person also has to have contact with or have a way to get access to all your files and get ahold of the contacts in your life if need be. That's a heavy choice. When you think about it, that is a lot to ask of someone. I changed my Facebook status that day to share with people the question that crossed my mind. Many friends posted on the status that I could use them as a contact. It was nice to see that and it feels good to have people care. Although I have to remind myself that those people have their own lives and half of them live out of state, most of which I haven't talked to in a very long time. That was a reminder that there will always be people willing to help but in the same token you have to remember that if the people who help you don't know the whole story, which most don't, then the help will be temporary because grief and suffering is a lot for a person to handle. This is especially true if they aren't 100% invested in your life as a family member or spouse should be. I ended up putting down the name of my aunt who was my stepfather's sister. It is a mouthful I know, but she was a woman who took me under her wing through it all regardless of our lack of blood relation.

Another struggle I faced was the lack of a stable address. Having a mailing address seems like something that is standard and simple. When I was a teenager I used the address at the insurance agency I worked at for a long time. When I was in high school, the mail I received at my adopted father and stepmother's home was always intercepted by my stepmother. I would have to wait for garbage day to come and I would leave the house at night to go look through the garbage. I would find letters from the people I met at church camps that I wrote back and forth. I would put together all the pieces from them getting ripped up and I would be able to read my mail that way. I would write these people back and I would bring the letters into work and mail the responses out to people from my work address. I would then make sure they had changed to writing me at my work address. When I lived with my mom and stepfather for that year, I had the same problem. My stepdad would get the letters that were mailed to me and keep them from me. He would tell me that if I let him take pictures of me he would give me my mail. I would go along with it and let him take the pictures so I could get the mail that was sent to me.

The time that I was married was the longest period of time that I had the same address. The period of time before that I rented homes and rooms from people so I never had a stable address for more than a three-month period. When my marriage ended and I rented a house, I changed everything to the rental home address. I had the realization that address also had a one-year shelf life. I am still very uncomfortable with this state of uncertainty. It would be nice to finally have a place to settle in and to never have to worry about a change of address again but that also seems like that is something that will never happen. That is just something that I will have to realize is an area where I will be different than the social norm of having a family to call home base. I had to accept that I won't have a safe address to have things sent to. In my opinion, it is better to expect for something to be out of reach because when it does become an option and is in reach hope is obtained and fulfilled. I don't believe in false hope, either. I believe that hope is hope whether it comes to pass or not. The act of being hopeful is a positive thing. Regardless of whether the situation ends up going well or not does not change the fact that for a period of time you held on to hope and happiness was present.

Chapter 13

Biological Brothers

Through all the tragedy in my life, I was still able to see that there was purpose in the midst of it all. Being adopted, I always wondered where the rest of my real family was. I wondered whether they knew about me and if the ones I had met previously even cared about me. I had always known of my biological father, mother and brother. I knew that my biological father was in Detroit and in a motorcycle club and I knew my mom was in prison because I got the secret collect calls from her throughout my childhood. I knew my brother and father best because they would come and visit me all throughout my childhood. I always wondered about who the rest of my family were and where they were. I hoped to one day make contact with all of them. The day the doors opened to meet more of my biological family was at my brother's funeral. That day I met my half-sister from my biological father's side. She was married and had a daughter. I also met my grandparents and biological aunt, all on my biological father's side. I kept in contact with that part of the family from that day forward and began to learn about my childhood during the days before I was adopted. I also learned more about my brother Brian through them. I took a trip down to Florida to visit my half sister from my biological fathers side and her family a year after my brother's funeral. That first trip is where our relationship began. I have been down to Florida five times to visit them since then and we keep in contact. To this day she is still a huge part of my life.

During one of the phone calls from my mother in prison, she had given me her father's name. She told me to contact him so I could find out about who my grandfather was. I searched online and found him. When I was 17, I flew down to Nashville to visit and established a relationship with him. I will write more about his part in my life later. My mother had also told me that I had a half brother that was five years younger than me and twin half brothers that were 13 years younger than I was. I contacted my younger brother and was able to meet him last year when he came to Michigan to visit me and then I flew down to Florida to visit him. That was an emotional meeting when he came to visit me in Michigan in more than one way. The day he came to Michigan happened to be the morning after my husband told me for the first time that he wanted to get a divorce. I was in a state of heartbreak. My biological half brother from my prison-bound mother's side had called me that day letting me know that he was in Michigan. He was there because his girlfriend had used him for a ride up from Orlando to see her family in Michigan. She dumped him when he brought her up and left him in a hotel he had booked for them to stay at. That was very hard for me to be supportive of him and stay strong without letting him know what was going on in my own life. I compartmentalized my feelings and my current life circumstances to be strong for him. I got to know a lot more about him that day and it was the first day that I met him in person. It was a big deal in my life at the time. He wanted me to take him to where I lived and he wanted to meet my husband and learn more about us. He had looked us both up on Facebook and saw that we were into riding dirt bikes and off-roading so he was really looking forward to hearing more about our life and to meeting my husband. I sent my husband a text telling him that I had just met up with my biological brother for the first time ever and that I was bringing him to the house. I told him that I didn't want him to know what was going on in our marriage. That was very hard for me to tell my brother all about my husband knowing that he technically wasn't going to ever see him again or get to know him in the future as my husband anymore. During that trip I grew to know him more and was able to encourage him in his current heartbreak. I fought back tears half the time because I was an internal emotional wreck facing my own devastation. The next year he invited me to meet his adopted family in Florida and they took me to Disney World for the first time. In November 2011, after finishing nursing school, I took a road trip to Florida to visit my mother in prison for the first time. That was an experience in itself. It was during that trip that I met my twin half-brothers for the first time. They were in a city a half hour away from the prison my mother was kept in.

The day I met my twin brothers I was staying at my husband's grandparents' house. I was very close with them and I would stay with them and visit them a lot. They played a huge supportive role in my life while I was married. They drove me to the house where the twins lived. Their home was only 20 minutes away from the Florida home that the grandparents lived in. When I arrived at the house, I knocked on the door and a little girl answered the door. There were many cars in the driveway that day. I found out that it was because the twins' father had just died that past week so there were many family members in town. When the little girl asked who I was, I heard an old woman's voice in the background saying "let her in, she is the twins' sister." As I walked in the door and looked over at their grandmother knitting in the corner, without even looking up she said "your mother said that you would come by one of these days when you were ready." With that statement, she yelled out for the boys to come to the living room. As the first boy came out, she said "boys, this is your sister." The first boy looked at me and didn't say a word. The second one came out and when I introduced myself and told them that their mom had a daughter and that was me, he ran back into his bedroom and shut the door. After a few minutes of silence mixed with small talk, the second boy came out and I began to talk to both of them.

While talking to the boys, they told me a story of how when my mom had been out of prison for a few months in the past year she took them to Busch Gardens. One of the boys said "she didn't like me." When I asked why he thought that he told me about how when she took the boys to Busch Gardens one of the boys annoyed her so much that when she entered the park she walked up to a guy that was standing by the bathrooms and gave him some money. She then took his number in exchange for him keeping her son for the day. Luckily the man returned her son to her at the end of the day. That paints a picture to you of the type of person my biological mother is. When I asked the grandmother if this was a true story she said that it was indeed true and that she will never let her see the boys again until it is their choice at age 18. I maintained contact with the boys and to this day I am still a part of their life.

Chapter 14

Death Exists

It has been said that with every goodbye you learn. I can definitely agree with that statement. I have seen a lot of loss in my life. I deal with it daily in the medical profession. Personal loss of those closest to us is what hurts the most. Some people lose their first loved one and they struggle to make it through the loss. Sometimes they have built up coping mechanisms. In some cases, they have placed emotional guards up to protect themselves. Some say that each loss gets easier. I cannot fully agree with that statement. A loss is a loss. When you lose someone close to you or someone you love, you are losing a part of yourself and a piece of your story. I have also learned that loss doesn't always come from death. There are more ways to lose people in your life aside from death. If a loved one goes to prison and you never get to see them again, it hurts the same. In situations like that it tends to be harder because there is no closure. People who keep close company with many people end up incurring a lot more loss than those who keep to themselves and don't invest in people. I often wonder which tragedy is worse, losing many friends because you had many friends or living life without having many friends at all in order to avoid the hurt of the loss. You have to come to a point where you realize that life is short and that we are not promised tomorrow. When you truly understand that, loss won't hurt as bad because you will be confident that you have spent your days wisely with the people placed in your life. Investing in people is my goal in life. I want people to remember me when I am gone as someone who lived life for others and not just for myself.

From my personal experience, I have found that I have a broad scope of friends from many different backgrounds. I have many different groups of people that have impacted and played a role in my life. I made a lot of connections with people living in different situations and areas my whole life. With that fact alone I have allowed myself the unavoidable openness to hurt. My family situation alone, having family spread all over the place, leaves me open for plenty of hurt. I am going to share with you some of that the losses I endured and learned from. The first loss was the death of my brother Brian. That was the hardest loss for me because of him being my only full biological sibling. Losing him at age 13, I felt that I had lost the potential to ever have a birth heritage of my own. At age 15, I lost my friend Keith on Christmas Eve. He was coming home to visit and he was killed in a car crash at the corner of our street. That same year a friend from school was shot at a local pizza store during a robbery. At age 16, I was taken from my dad's place and moved in with my adopted mother and stepfather where I was thrown into the new school where all contact of my past life was completely cut off. I was forced into making new friends. I played soccer and made a friend who became my running partner. At our first game in March, I remember standing on the sideline with her and we were talking about death. It was a cold night game and snow began to fall but the game went on. During our conversation I remember Shauna saying that if she died she would want to be so cold that she didn't feel any pain. When that game ended I was about to jump in a car with her and head to McDonald's with the team but our coach asked me to ride with him so he could talk to me about some things from the game. That night, Shauna didn't make it to McDonald's. I remember getting the phone call that night at 3 am. Our coach called me to let me know that Shauna had died instantly in a car crash on the way to McDonald's. They had to use the jaws of life to get her out of the vehicle. We had passed the accident on the way to the restaurant but didn't recognize it as her car. I was supposed to be in the car with her that night and I see the circumstances that specifically pulled me away from that car. I believe that is another example of a higher purpose and plan for my life.

The following week after Shauna's death, the high school was an emotional wreck. There were grief counselors set up and the soccer team met in the conference room in the principal's office to debrief. I will never forget my friend Noble sitting in the office entrance and as I walked by he asked me why I was so upset. I remember being so angry at him for questioning me. I remember fondly the words he spoke to me. He said "Rachel, she is gone now and death happens. It is a part of life and at some point you need to move on and realize that death is inevitable and it will happen to all of us." I walked past him with such resentment and I refused to sit with him at lunch like usual that week. I even refused to go with him to the pond party at our friend's farm that he invited me to that weekend. I got a call from his mother the day of the pond party telling me that he had been in a drowning accident at our friend's pond and that he was in the hospital in critical condition. Before I made it to the hospital I got the phone call that he had not made it and that I didn't need to come up to the hospital anymore. Those two deaths happened in my first year at a new school and two of my closest friends were taken from me. I was a wreck and at that point I questioned God and the purpose of life. What helped me through both of them was remembering the words that Noble had spoken to me after Shauna's death. He had spoken truth to me. At the time I didn't understand and I was angry. I reflected on the words he spoke in order to cope. In those situations, my stepfather was so cruel that he told me I wasn't allowed to go to the funerals. I had to sneak out of the second story window and have a friend pick me up in order to take me to each of the funerals. After Noble's funeral, I didn't go back home for a few days because I was afraid of the repercussions that were in store for me. Eventually I had to go back and face that situation. As you have already read in previous chapters, the results were not desirable.

When I came back to my adopted father's home for my senior year, there was a man that stood in as a father figure for me. I met him through a friend I made when I was at the new school the past year. He was in his late 50's. He would pick me up in a parking lot at the corner of my adopted dad's street and take me for dinner on the back of his motorcycle. We would hang out with his girlfriend at the restaurant where she worked. He taught me so much about life. He encouraged me and inspired hope. Three years ago he died of brain cancer and all I was left with from him were the inspirations and hope he gave to me when I needed encouragement. I look back at the memories of him and I am thankful for the time he was in my life and the days that he showed me light and hope in the midst of darkness. He was only in my life for a season. With that, I learned that even if people are only given to us for a short period in our lives, there is a reason they were there. We can't let the time we are given with people go to waste. We need to seek out the reason and purpose and we need to let the influence live out in our lives. When I turned 18, I had gotten into riding motorcycles myself. That year, I started dating a guy who rode a motorcycle as well. After the third date I got a phone call from his brother that he had died in a motorcycle crash on the way home. That same summer after getting into the sport bike scene I lost 3 friends in bike crashes. I remember watching my friend Bryan get hit by a Blazer and as I saw his body fly through the air I was reminded of how short life is. As I ran to him on the side of the road and tried to keep him conscious, I watched the blood flow out of his ears. He took his last breath during a final attempt to spit out the blood that was filling his mouth. I could not even ride my bike home that night. I was a wreck and it took me a while to get back on a bike again after that accident.

The point with that is that eventually I did get back on. To this day I still ride my motorcycle. It was a traumatic event. To this day I still get flashbacks of that moment when I saw him fly through the air. I realize that there is nothing I can do to change the situations now and there is nothing I could have done at the time to prevent that from happening. Part of me still tells myself that there was something I could have done to prevent it. There is a part of that story that is hard for me to live with. Part of me blames myself for Bryan's death that day. I had invited a girlfriend to come out with us that evening. She was running late. It was dark out. As her blazer turned left into the parking lot she struck the right side of his motorcycle and that was the impact that cost Bryan his life. I still struggle with that and blame myself for making the phone call to invite her out. But that is something I have to remind myself is unpredictable and it was not purposeful. In a situation like that, it is hard to not blame yourself. I blamed myself for a long time afterwards.

When I was 22 years old, I got a phone call from a lady at the office I worked at. She had told me that my manager's son had just overdosed on heroin and died. With that phone call, I was put into shock. I had become close with him through the years. He was only a year younger than I was. The shoelaces in my shoes I had on that day I got the phone call were the ones he had put on for me. He was the only one I knew that could lace my skateboarding shoes the right way. I thought back to the times we had spent time together and talked about life. I remembered the days I took him to church with me. He would tell me about how lost he felt he was in life and how he was fighting his addictions but felt he couldn't win and how he felt his family was so disappointed in him all the time. In his case, his addiction won. His mother was my manager at the time. I had lived with them off and on so I looked at him as a brother. She would update us at work daily on his rehab experiences and how well he had been doing. This came to us all as a shock because he had been doing so well. At his funeral I saw his friends, who were devastated. They all felt guilt and shame. They all had intentions of getting clean after seeing what the end result of one mistake can be. With that loss, I was again dealing with the loss of a friend. At the same time, my manager was dealing with the loss of a son. Through that I learned that one loss can mean many things to many people and people grieve differently. I also learned through that loss that our decisions affect more than just ourselves.

Last year, my best friend Anna was found with a suicide letter next to her body. She and I got into a fight and didn't talk for several months. She had tried to contact me and I ignored her phone calls and text messages because I was trying to prove a point. She had a drinking problem and I couldn't support her habit anymore, so I was playing tough love in our friendship. She was a model and one of the most beautiful girls I knew. She had gotten dressed in a beautiful red dress that she bought when we had gone shopping together and she put on her makeup and got her nails done at the salon that day. Her hair was perfectly curled as always. She had used her boyfriend's gun to shoot herself while he was in the room next to her. That loss was hard for me to deal with because I struggled with the fact that I wasn't there for her when she needed me and that I should have been a better friend, knowing she struggled with depression.

Just a week before writing this chapter, I got a message letting me know that my teenage sweetheart from my year living with my adopted mother and stepfather had been killed in a car crash this past weekend. Devastation is an understatement. With that phone call, I made the mistake of reading that message while working in the emergency room. That was a rough day at work but also reminded me that this was my life now and I had patients to take care of who were struggling for their own lives. When I got a call this week again with bad news it was a friend from my father's biker club letting me know that someone very close to me had died in a bike wreck on the way back from our friend's wedding. He had just won the motorcycle in a raffle a few days back and he took it out on the first ride to this wedding. A deer hit him. I was devastated. He played the role of a big brother to me after Brian died. He looked out for me and made sure that I was safe in any situation I entered into. Losing him was really hard and it will be a hard loss to cope with. These are just some examples of some of the losses I went through in 5 years' time. There are different types of loss. There are losses from death and there are also losses from separation or removal. Each has a void and each leaves an empty space that can either be filled or left alone and worked around.

Chapter 15

Grandfather Time

The chapter you are about to read took me weeks to bring myself to begin writing. I have a voice recorder that I talk into to remind myself of stories that I plan to write about. The voice recording for this chapter was an hour long and I was in tears half the time that I recorded it. My feelings were poured into that recording. The last thing I wanted to put myself through was feeling those emotions again. For the purpose of writing this book, I knew that the recording had to be listened to in order to recall details. I still can't believe that I went through this situation. It takes listening to myself speak to remember and acknowledge that this really did happen. Although now I can say that the process of writing out my recording was actually very therapeutic. The story that I brought myself to listen to in order to write this chapter was the story of my biological grandfather. I was not aware of who my biological grandfather was until I was 17 years old and my biological mother in prison called me to tell me the full name of who my grandfather was in order to look him up and get in touch with him. This was the father of my biological mother who had been in and out of prison my whole life. I searched his name and found him on the internet. I began calling his number daily with no response. One day he picked up and the first words he said were "who is this?" At that point, I introduced myself. I told him that his daughter had a child 17 years ago and that was who I was. He acknowledged that he heard about me before from my mother and didn't believe he would ever hear from me. That day we talked for two hours on the phone catching up on life and telling stories. We kept in contact the years following through letters, email and phone conversations. He was the one who bought me my first laptop when I went away to college at age 17. Our relationship grew and he told me all the time that he was so proud of me. He told me that I was the only one in his life that he could trust. He told me that I was the only positive person in his life that he could be proud of.

He flew me down to Nashville to visit him twice that first year. I can still remember walking out of baggage claim and scanning the room for his face. I remember seeing an old man standing there holding a sign with my name on it. It was just like the movies. Although, I will admit that the first hug that day was quite awkward. It was the feeling of finally finding a piece of your history mixed with embracing a total stranger in your arms. The first time I went down to Nashville, he drove me through the city. He showed me all the places he had lived. He told me stories of the three wives he had in the past. He told me about my grandmother, who had committed suicide due to struggling with depression. He said it was mainly from her daughter's, aka my mother's, lifestyle. He told me about his three children. He told me stories of my mother when she was growing up and about his two sons that he had no interest in having a relationship with. He told me stories about my brother Brian and the hurt he had felt when he was murdered. He told me about his days in the military. He showed me pictures and memory books.

His house was dark and smoky. That part of the experience made me very uncomfortable because I don't like being around smoke. He always had a pipe in his mouth. The curtains on all of the windows were always drawn because he didn't want anyone looking in his house. The more I observed around his house, I learned more about him and his fears. He had stacks of bulk food in the corner and stacks of bottled water. He only left the house when necessary to get food to stock up on because he was always afraid of getting robbed. He had been taken advantage of by his previous wives and also by his own kids. He told me stories about how one son asked him for money every month and that the other one would ask for a check and then call and say he never got it. When he would send him another one my grandfather would see that both checks had been deposited. Hearing these stories, I can understand why he didn't want to maintain a relationship with any of his children. That son who pulled the check scams was in and out of jail often, just like my mother. Then there was my mother who was always in and out of jail. She was always asking for money and anything else she could get her hands on from him. His own children had used him and betrayed him. I could understand why he lived the life of a hermit. He was scared of everything and thought that everyone was out to get him. He believed everyone was after his money.

I was the only person in his life that my grandfather trusted. I was the only person in his family that even knew where he lived. I was the only person who had ever been allowed in his house. Looking back now, I can see that was a really big deal to him. I feel honored that he allowed me into his life. He had set me up a room in his basement for when I would come down to visit him. He even bought me my own sheet set for the bed downstairs with zoo animals on it. I would visit a couple times each year. We maintained a relationship and it gave me direction and hope knowing that there was someone else out there that was truly my blood relative. I had a heritage again and I felt security in that. I had found someone else in life that was my own blood and who truly cared about me. Over time, we had gotten to the point of talking every week. He was so proud of me being in nursing school and he was so excited for me to graduate. He never came to visit me in Michigan because he was afraid of leaving the house and he had a fear of flying. He told me that he wouldn't be coming to my graduation but he made sure I knew how proud he was of me.

During the summer months of 2010, he started telling me in our phone conversations that he wasn't feeling good lately and that he had been getting dizzy spells and passing out in his house. Hearing that worried me, so I began to talk to him everyday. I looked forward to our conversations because he had a lot of wisdom to offer me and I learned a lot about him and his life journeys. Eventually, he started going to the doctor's to get tests done because his medical condition was getting worse. I asked him if I could come spend the summer with him and he told me he was in such bad shape that he didn't want me to see him like this until he got healthy again and he would tell me to just focus on school. He had been getting rides to and from the appointments from his neighbor. He was to the point where he was using a motorized scooter at home to get around and to even get the mail. He tried to make the best of that situation by telling me that he was going to get a bigger motor for the scooter and start racing it and building jumps in the backyard. I took the humor as his way of coping.

He was having different tests and procedures done and he would tell me about them. He told me he was getting weak and that his skin had turned a yellowish color this past week. The diagnostic testing continued but he would not tell me the results. He told me he was getting a bile duct drain put in that week. I put two and two together with my knowledge of being in nursing school. I asked him what his diagnosis was. When I asked him that question he was very hesitant to tell me. I remember driving on the freeway to my summer class and telling him that he has to stop hiding it and that he had to tell me what was wrong. Finally he admitted that the doctor had told him that he was very sorry to let him know but that he had developed pancreatic cancer. At that point, I lost it. I was in tears instantly because from studying nursing, I knew the percentages of survival rate with pancreatic cancer. I had to pull off the highway and stop for a few minutes to cry as I finished the conversation with him. He kept telling me that it was not a big deal and that there was treatment for it and we could figure something out together to get him better. He said that it was stage four but that he was still hopeful. Him being confident did not help me because I was looking at the physical side of it with my medical background. I knew that it was not a hopeful situation.

I was late to class that day and I sat outside the door of the room in tears, not having the strength to go in because I knew my classmates were in there preparing for the test that I was supposed to be taking that day. My college professor walked past to go into the room with the copies of the test and he stopped and asked what was wrong. When I told him the situation he sat down next to me and shared his story with me. He told me about how he himself had been diagnosed with pancreatic cancer this past year and he had the Whipple procedure done. He said that now the cancer was gone and he just has to get checked every 6 months. That day I found hope because I felt that God sent him to calm my spirits and to motivate me in helping my grandfather find a cure. I was able to go into class that day and take my exam. I struggled through the answers with tears in my eyes but maintained the strength to get through the exam. I called my grandfather that day and told him that I was going to do some research and that we were going to beat this together through prayer and medical research. He made me promise him that I would not tell anyone at all what was going on and that his children were never to find out. That was a hard secret for me to keep. It was a very hard emotional process to rationalize why I wasn't letting anyone know. Somehow I found the strength to keep the promise. I had to keep it a secret anyway because I was the only person he had in his life to trust. We began to talk even more and he would call me to tell me about things he wanted done if he did pass on. He would tell me to get out paper to write down his last wishes. Those were hard conversations to have with him but I knew that he had no one else to talk to about it. I had to be strong and agree to honor his wishes. I fought back the tears as I wrote down his wishes in a notebook.

Chapter 16

The Heritage Dies

At the beginning of July, I started to get no answer when calling him. This was very unusual given the time we usually spent on the phone. The first 3 days I thought that maybe he was just tired and needed rest. But then the following day I called to tell him happy 4th of July and there was no answer again. I began to get worried. I needed advice. I drove to my friend Eric's home and talked with him and his family about it. From there, I decided that I needed to find out what was going on. I called a local church in the town my grandfather lived in and I talked to the pastor. I told the man the situation and asked him if he could make a house call to my grandfather's home to see if he would answer the door for him. The pastor told me that he would be able to stop by to visit my grandfather the following morning. I was relieved for a moment but then I couldn't stand waiting and not knowing what was going on until the next morning. That was too long to sit and wait. I then looked up his address on Google maps and I located the addresses of his neighbors. I searched them online to get the phone numbers. I called them both. Neither one had answered the phone call. This time I was desperate.

I called a local Nashville pizza shop near his home and I ordered a pizza. I paid over the phone and had it delivered to my grandfather's house in Nashville. The pizza delivery driver called my number and said that she had been knocking at my door and wondered why I wasn't answering. At that point I told the girl what was going on and that I would tip her well. I told her that I wanted her to do me a favor. She was hesitant, but I assured her again that I would tip her well. I asked her to try the back door and she said that also was closed and that she got no answer. I then asked her to go to the mailbox and tell me the date of the last piece of mail that was in there. She did so hesitantly. She told me that the last piece was from five days ago. At that point I knew there was something wrong. I then had the girl walk to the neighbor's house and give them the pizza. At that time I told her to give the neighbor my phone number and have them call me. I was so thankful that girl was willing to help me out the way she did. I made sure that she was well taken care of.

When the neighbor called me, I had them walk over to the other neighbor's home who had been taking my grandfather to his appointments. I asked her to hand him the phone. When I spoke with him he said the last time that he had spoken with my grandfather was a week ago when he brought him a meal and he refused it. That day my grandfather told him to leave him alone. Neither of them had seen him around since last week. Next, I had them go to the front door and try to knock. They were both on speakerphone with me at that point. They said that the door was locked but not fully closed and they said they were able to push the door open. I instructed them not to go in because I knew that my grandfather was very paranoid and carried a gun with him at all times. I asked them to just shout into the house to see if they got a response. I heard from the background my grandpa yelling "leave me alone." With that response, I knew that my grandfather was still alive. From hearing his voice I knew that something just wasn't right.

At that point, I made the decision that I needed to leave right then and drive straight to Nashville. I left my friend Eric's house and headed straight to Nashville. I got there early in the morning at 6 am. As I walked into the house, I told him that it was his granddaughter coming into his house and that I would be walking towards his bedroom. I wanted to give him warning of who I was so he didn't think someone was breaking in. I leaned up against the wall outside his bedroom. I was silent for a moment listening for sounds to the left of me from his bedroom. I could hear him groaning so I knew he was alive and that he was still in there. I was breathing slow and staying as still as possible knowing that he had a gun and that the moment I turned the corner it could have been my last breath if I startled him. As I turned the corner and announced again who I was, I saw him lying in his bed covered in blood and urine. There were pills all over the floor and the floor was soaking wet. In that moment he raised his hand with his gun and pointed it right at me. I took a deep breath and I told him once more that it was his granddaughter and that I got in because his front door was open. I told him to put the gun down and that everything would be ok. When he realized who I was he moaned and asked me how I had gotten in. He asked me why I was there and not in school. I explained to him why I came down. He kept saying he didn't want me to see him like this and that he wanted me to go back to finish school. I told him that I was there now and I was going to take care of him.

I got him cleaned up and changed the sheets in his bed and sat him up in bed. I asked him why there were pain pills all over and he said that he hasn't been able to get out of bed for the past few days and he didn't have water because he knocked over the pitcher. He said that every time he tried to get a pill, it fell on the floor and he didn't have the strength to get them. His pain was intense and his skin was completely jaundiced. So much so, that even his eyes were yellow. He had lost a lot of weight and you could see his bones through his skin. He had soaked himself in his own urine and the drain he had in his side from a procedure had leaked blood and bile all over him. The first thing I did was give him water and his pain medication. We began to talk about what was going on. He was in disbelief and kept saying that he was just sick and believed he would get better soon. He made me promise again that I would not call any of his children and tell them what was going on. He said he did not want to go to the hospital and that he wanted everyone to leave him alone at this point. He agreed to let me stay and I assured him I would be taking care of him. He was in and out of delirium that day as the pain and cancer took over his body. I slept in the room across the hall from him. Through the night I would try to give him his pain medications but it was not working. He was not able to swallow very well. I laid in the bedroom across the hall listening to the cries, groans and screams of pain. I felt helpless because there was nothing I could do to control the pain. I could not sleep knowing the agony he was in only feet away from where I was lying. I went in to his room and laid down next to him and hugged him.

I could not fight back the tears at that point. As we both cried, I told him that I didn't know what to do or how to handle this. I felt helpless. I felt like I was abandoning him in some way just by being there unable to help him any further. I had no one to turn to. I had no direction on even what I should do. I told him that I felt like it was time to notify his family. He yelled and me and said "you promised you wouldn't tell my kids!" At that moment I knew that I needed to figure something out because his condition was declining and I didn't know what else to do. At that time I was still married, so I tried to call my husband for guidance and to have someone to talk to. He was in Colorado at that time with one of his girlfriends on a hiking trip so I wasn't able contact him. I don't communicate with my adopted family so that was out of the question. They didn't even know that I had this grandfather in Nashville. So I tried to contact my in-laws but they were all up at their family cottage that weekend for vacation. I was left with no resources and no contacts so I had to figure it out alone.

That next morning, I looked through his files and I found long term care benefit information and his insurance paperwork. I began to call around to the companies and find out if he had home care coverage and what the options were. My grandfather had told me that he wanted to stay at home and not go to the hospital. I was trying to honor that. I got ahold of a home hospice company and they sent a social worker and a home health nurse out to my grandfather's house. I told them the situation while we were in the kitchen before they went in to assess my grandfather. I went alone into the bedroom he was in to tell him that a visiting nurse was coming in to assess his pain level to get something that would work for his pain. It wasn't the truth but I knew it was the only way to get a stranger into his bedroom. He agreed to let her come in to his room. After talking with the social worker and nurse after the assessment they thought it was best to get him into a hospice facility where he could get better cared for. They told me that his case was too complex to stay comfortable at home. The problem was that they needed a signature from a family member in order to take him to a facility. They went in the room with me and talked to my grandfather about a power of attorney. Since the social worker was a notary, my grandfather signed over power of attorney to me that day. At that point the pressure was on. I was now in charge of the decision making and all the plans and paperwork and finances that needed to be taken care of. I agreed to let an ambulance pick him up to take him to a medical center.

When the ambulance came to transport my grandfather to the hospice facility, I had to convince him that we were only leaving the house for a doctor's appointment but that we would be coming back home. He agreed but with hesitancy. It took four people to lift him onto the chair to take him out of the house. As he was being backed into the ambulance he looked up at me as I stood behind the ambulance watching him get loaded into the back. I told him I would be following right behind him. At that point he looked at me and a tear ran down his cheek and he said "we aren't coming back are we?" That was the first time I ever saw my grandfather cry. I ignored the statement, afraid to hurt him by answering truthfully. I told him that we were going to make him feel better and reassured him that I would be right behind the ambulance. That was one of the hardest moments and one of the traumatizing visuals that I cannot get out of my mind to this day.

When we got him to the facility and to his room, I had to speak for him as his power of attorney and I had to make medical decisions for him. I had never been in this position before and I was unsure how to handle it. To the best of my knowledge and to the best of his wishes, I signed the papers and I made the decisions. Signing the do not resuscitate order and the order to stop treatment as his organs began to fail was hardest for me because I knew that is what he said he wanted but at the same time in my selfishness I was not ready to lose him or to face another death. I sat down next to him on his hospital bed. I explained to him that they were going to put him on a pain pump and they were going to get him settled in. I remember telling him that I would keep the promise not to tell the family but that it was really hard for me to be making these decisions for him. He told me that he was not upset with me for bringing him there and that he wanted me to leave him at that point and head back to Detroit so that I wouldn't miss my tests at school. I told him that I would figure it out and that he didn't need to worry about it. As we talked that day, he began to fade away more and more as each hour passed by. His sentences weren't making sense and eventually he stopped talking and did not open his eyes again.

I stayed with him again that night. The hospice nurses brought a cot in the room for me to sleep next to him. At night I would lie down next to him. I held his hand, read the bible to him and sang him songs throughout the night. Each time he cringed with pain, I pushed the button for him so he would get more pain meds. I struggled with that, thinking that it was my fault he couldn't talk to me. I thought maybe I was giving him too much pain medication. I realize now that I did the right thing because he needed to be comfortable. It would have been selfish for me to allow him to be in pain just so that I could talk with him. Through the nights, he would have night terrors. I believe they were flashbacks from the wars he fought in. I would reorient him and tell him that I was there with him. He would grab ahold of my hand and calm back down. I stayed with him two nights there and I was scared to leave during the day because I didn't want him to be alone. I would stay there at the hospital with no food, dreading what was about to come. On Sunday morning, when I woke up, the doctor came in to assess him and he told me that my grandfather's respiratory patterns had changed to apneic breathing and that his skin was beginning to mottle. My grandfather was no longer able to squeeze my hand anymore. The doctor told me that it didn't look like he would make it through the rest of the day.

I got a call that morning from the pastor that I had called before heading to Nashville. He asked how my grandfather was doing. I told him that it wasn't good so that pastor whom I had never met told me that he would have his church praying for the situation during their church service. He told me they would be praying for my strength through this difficult time. Having that pastor call me was a blessing I didn't expect. It was another reminder that I wasn't alone. It was nice to know that there were people praying for me through this. I asked the doctor to step out of the room and I got into the bed with him to lay down next to him. I rested my head on his chest and began to cry. I told him how much he meant to me how much I loved him and that I wasn't mad at him. I promised him that I would go back and finish nursing school and I told him that everything was going to be ok and that he shouldn't be scared to die. After that statement I heard through his chest each heartbeat get farther and farther apart until he took his final gasp of air. He let the last breath out and another heartbeat did not come. I spent the following moments weeping and mourning his death. I sank my head into his shoulder and cried. I was devastated and didn't know what to do or who to call or how I was supposed to handle this. I knew that I had to pick my chin up and move on because with death there is a process afterwards. I dried my tears and I left the room after I pulled myself together. I brought the doctor back in who then called the time of death.

They began to prepare my grandfather's body. I left the room and went to the waiting room to cry every last tear I held in my body.

Chapter 17

The Estate

After I spent some time with my grandfather, I went to the desk to talk to the social worker, nurses and care manager about where my grandfather was going now. They told me that only the plans I had set up with the crematory had been finalized but that at that point I no longer had power of attorney since he was deceased. They said that the process now was that they needed to speak to the next of kin. That would be his oldest son. I was torn at that point because I had found their contact information in his paperwork but I had honored my grandfather's wishes and I had not contacted any of them in the past months to even tell them he was sick. I had never even met his sons, so they had no idea who I was. I remembered my grandfather talking about his will and that the executor would take care of the details so that I wouldn't have to. I remember him trying to tell me about where the will was located in his storm shelter but I had put that thought behind me and didn't put two and two together to go and get it. I had no idea who the executor was and I had no idea who I was supposed to call. I didn't know what to do. It was a Sunday afternoon at this point and I was stuck. He was gone. I had no one to contact and all I had was the numbers of his children that I had found in his office. I had a test Monday morning for nursing school. I had promised him I would go home and take it. I had to make the decision in that moment. Once they took his body away, no matter how much hurt I was in, I promised him that I would go back and finish school. There was nothing more I could do at that point. I went back to his house locked it up and I put a note for the executor on the table letting them know where I hid his gun. I wrote in the note where his wallet was and where his money was kept. I left that night and drove through the night to make it to class in the morning to take my exam as I had promised. I gave the neighbors my number so that they could contact me with any updates.

Afterwards I got a call from the crematory asking when the next of kin would be coming to finalize details because they had no record of me being family due to the name change in the adoption and then the marriage name. At that point I knew I needed to make some phone calls. I first called Florida State Prison and notified them to tell my mother that her father had died. She called me shortly after. The first question she asked was "did you find the will?" I was disgusted but I was not shocked. I told her to figure out a way to notify her other brother and told her that I would call the oldest. The next phone call I made was to the oldest son. That was a hard call to make. I first told him who I was. I told him about how his father had gotten sick and then I told him what had happened. He began to cry and yell and he was so angry with me for not telling him. He called me "little orphan Annie" and told me to stay out of things. I called the crematory and they said they heard from the son now and they were not able to tell me anything else at that point. From then on it was out of my hands and all I had written down for my grandfather's wishes at that point meant nothing.

The next day I got a phone call from the neighbor that took my grandfather to his appointments. He told me that there was a man crawling through my grandfather's window and that he saw him walk out of the house putting things in his car. He told me that he had a stack of papers with him as he walked out of the storm shelter. At that point, it all made sense when my grandfather was talking to me about going to the storm shelter and at the time I just brushed it off. At that moment, I knew it was the will my grandpa told me to go and get. My grandfather had made a new will leaving his children out of it and he had it at home and never had it turned in because he didn't expect to get so sick so fast. That is what the son had walked out with that day. To this day that will has not been found and all that I know of what was written in it comes from the stories that the neighbor told me from the car rides he took with my grandfather to and from appointments and to and from the lawyer's office. The final step of turning the will in to his lawyer was never done because my grandfather never had the chance to turn it in after he got sick.

The house was emptied out and the will he had made in 1999 was the only one that was located after the executor was finally notified. My grandfather turned out to be a very wealthy man. I would have never guessed how much money he had with the way he lived. It does make sense to me now why he was so scared with the sheltered way he lived. When the will was settled, all three children were given their portion. Two of the children were in prison at the time. My mother was released from prison shortly after the funds were given to her and she used it to get right back into drugs and as of this past year she has bought herself another 7 years in prison. The hardest part of that situation was not the fact that the new will was stolen by one of his children. The hardest part is that nothing that he had wished for came true. Everything he feared and was afraid of took place and that was hard for me to watch knowing the details that surrounded it. To this day I have no idea where his ashes are and his gravestone he had picked out still has no home. The half-brother I had met in Florida asked me what cemetery he was in so that he could go visit. I didn't have an answer for him. His remains will never be honored or placed where he had chosen. That is one of the hardest situations I have faced. I had to go through it alone. I lost my heritage that day. I lost the only person who knew about my true biological history.

Chapter 18

Resilience

Through all those trials I wrote about, somehow I still managed to graduate college and become a registered nurse working a full time job. I no longer have to work 4 part time jobs at once and sleep in a car between shifts just to make it to my next job. I have arrived. I finished school. I have my career. It took hard work and dedication. I spent my time in waitressing and I used my smile and charm for bigger tips. I put my time in as a pizza delivery driver. I answered phones. I filed papers. I cleaned houses. I went through the labor to get here. I am not saying that it is easy. I am telling you that it is possible. There are people who get to where I am today because everything was easy and it was always handed to them. That is not the fault of those people. Good for them. It is nice to know that some people have good parents who help them succeed. That is a good thing! This book is to open their eyes to see what goes on in other situations and it is to show those less fortunate as I was, that it doesn't matter what your surroundings are like, all that matters is how badly you yourself want to succeed.

With my story and all that I faced, I still managed to finish school, get my degree, and maintain health, both mental and physical. Most importantly, I am still alive! After psychiatrists, medications, illness, suicide attempts, and mental institutions, I made it out alive. It hurt going through it and I thought I would never make it through. It was a matter of getting up each time I fell and moving a little faster each time knowing that discouragement and regret were chasing after me. I moved onward and I looked upward. I learned which bridges I needed to burn in order to force myself to never go back. I also learned which bridges to reinforce in order to make sure they never fall.

When a child falls off their bicycle and scrapes their elbow, they will run into the house crying to their dad. Sometimes the dad has to remind them that the scar will always be there but now the bleeding has stopped and there is a bandage to help healing. At some point, you need to stop crying. The child has to realize that just because there is a scar there, doesn't mean that it hurts anymore. Crying at the time of the incident is natural but to continue crying just because it happened even though the pain is gone is not normal. With the trials in life we need to let the "bandage" cover our wounds as they heal so that when it comes off and the temporary fix to our problem goes away, we can look at the scar the injury left and learn to avoid what caused it. Then we can understand that healing does come and the scars are meant to tell a story.

For some people, the temporary bandage in the analogy may refer to a new friend that we meet. To some, it may be alcohol and then a drinking problem begins. To some, it may be a new addiction that hides the pain. To others it may mean ignoring the problem. The part we have to realize is that the bandage is temporary to cover our wounds. At some point, that bandage will need to come off. At some point, the temporary fixes we found for the problem will go away. That is the point where we will need to decide if looking at the scar left will ruin our lives or if we will use it for good. We have to make the decision. Our temporary fixes buy us time but they won't help us make the decision. The advice we get from friends or counselors won't make the decision for us. We have to purpose in our minds how the next chapter will play out. We get to decide. That is the beauty of autonomy. So often people let others decide for them. Sometimes we just go with the normal chapter that follows and take that as how it is supposed to be. A person who lives that way will never move forward in life. That person will never become anything more in life if they don't personally want to and make the decision to do so. Some people like to sit there and cry on the pavement while the wound is open because to them that is the only way they can get attention from people. That is not a healthy way to live because that also is a temporary bandage that will go away in time. I made it through the trials in my life because I learned that temporary fixes were always gone at the end of the day. I learned that the only person who would ever take care of me is myself. Each person has to take the responsibility of the outcomes from the decisions in his own life. No one else will ever care as much about you as you should care about yourself. That doesn't mean that you are selfish. That means that you are taking the steps necessary to make yourself whole. How do you expect to ever help anyone else if you can't even help yourself? You can't give another person what you personally don't even have.

As a single woman, now looking back, I see how my life has progressed and how it has all worked together to get me to this point that I am at today. It is hard being single again because having a divorce on my record hurts enough. I still struggle with the thought that I may end up single for the rest of my life because I feel like no one will want to take on my emotional struggles and the burdens I will carry from my past. These are all lies that we believe that we need to overcome. It is one thing to maintain sanity while being single and accept singleness in life, but it is not okay to expect it as the only option. That is only self-doubt. You must realize that being alone does not mean that you are lonely. It is true that your past does not have to define your future. It is also true that the past does exist. Until you acknowledge the past that you have been through you can't understand where you are going. You can't fix a problem that you keep denying you have. I prefer to refer to myself as being "single again" rather than "divorced." I had to get into the mindset of going out on dates again. Learning to date again was hard. I have a story that scares people and I had to learn when to filter to not scare people away at the beginning before they even got to know me. I have always been very open about my story in life. On the dating scene it is hard to hold back your story and not tell people who you are and where you have been in life because that is the point of dating someone. You date someone to get to know them. It is a hard balance for me because if I tell people right away after one or two dates they freak out and I never hear from them again. Some are fine until the point when I tell them who my biological father is. Others slowly fade and feed me the cliché "you deserve better," line. But on the other hand, if you get close enough to someone and invest enough time into them to the point where you are ready to tell them the past behind the smile, then it hurts even more when they walk away from the relationship after you tell them about your past. That makes it hard to know when to speak up and when not to. To this day I have not had anyone stick around after they heard my story.

This may sound like a soap opera dilemma but this is my real life and it's another battle in life I have to face. It is a real concern and it hurts. I know I can't be the only one out there who faces this problem. That brings up the point again that we are never alone. There is always someone who faces the same trials we do. It tends to come in different forms but the hurt is still the same. If it isn't people running from me because I was previously married, it is because of who my biological father is and the crowd I am associated with through him. That deters a lot of people. It also determines sometimes who I can and cannot hang out with or date due to the fact that with any organization there are "opposing teams." It seems to be my luck to find people on the "opposing team" that I have to walk away from to avoid problems in that area.

That dilemma I just wrote about just goes along with the purpose of why I am writing this book. We are all human. We live life together. Our paths all intertwine and everyone you walk past has their own story and their own fears. We are not alone. We all have a lot more in common than we may think and the fact that someone else out there knows your hurt can comfort some, yet others fear it and want nothing to do with another individual that shares the same traumatic stories. One thing I believe is important to take away from reading this book is that community is critical. To have someone come beside you and tell you that you are not alone can make all the difference in your world. To have someone who suffered as you did come and lend you a hand or give you a word of wisdom or walk you through a problem, makes the trial they went through worth it. When you stand up after you go through a trial you are now equipped with the tools to help someone else behind you. It is how life should be. Life is hard and we all know that. Hiding our past only hurts us because we can't open up to anyone. We will never trust anyone and we lose the opportunity to help another person struggling to get through the same situation.

The only thing that helped me were the people placed in my path that I believe were sent by God at just the right times. People came along exactly when I needed them. I look back and see that I was never alone. Whether it was the true comfort I felt in my soul or the warmth of a hand on my back as I cried and someone telling me they had been there, too. That is true community; a non-judgmental atmosphere where people believe in walking with each other through life's trials. It is the circle of life. The same person that lends a hand to you through something will need your hand to help them through something else. We all go through trials at various points. The only question is when will you be the helper and when will you be the one who needs help? Everybody has his or her own story and experience. The struggles may be different but the hurt is the same.

I made it through the trials in life that have come so far. That does not mean for a second that they do not affect me still. I have many scars. Some are physical but many are emotional. I have learned that the emotional scars and pains hurt more than the physical ones. They are also the ones that can be hidden better with no outside support. While writing this book, I ended up on the floor near the point of tears almost every time I added to it. I had to acknowledge that these things happened in my life and they affect me, but I reminded myself that they do not define me. Even this past week, I had to write my mother a letter in prison asking her to stop sending me letters. I told her that during this sentence she was facing I was going to let her ride out the 7 years alone. I told her I wouldn't support her anymore. She was not fulfilling any part of me. She was draining me. That woman is persistent though. I can definitely see parts of her in myself and I can choose which traits of hers I will claim. This past Sunday I got a voicemail from a girl in North Dakota that I have never met telling me that she got my number from her mom in prison who is cell mates with my mother and she wanted me to know that my mom really wanted to make contact with me again.

As I listened, the thought crossed my mind of why I am in this situation and if this was really happening. Then I thought about how this random girl must have felt by calling a stranger as a favor to her mother that is currently in prison as well. What I took from that situation is that now I have a new contact of someone I can relate to and we may be able to help each other by sharing our stories. I plan on reaching out to her and looking at that situation with optimism. Sometimes I get lonely and I get scared of being alone. I sometimes wonder if I will ever have anyone in my life that will love me. I still face the same questions that you are asking yourself. I personally choose to move past that and make my own future and set my own goals regardless of the social norms. I have learned to be resilient and live life looking towards the future. It needs to happen whether I am single or if I have a companion. I live intentionally. Each day I make it a goal to help another person. Doing so, I find purpose and worth in life. It makes my trials valid. Each day I have to remind myself that I have come a long way and that my life has a purpose. Each day I seek to find that purpose. It is a daily choice.

The thing about resilience is that it is necessary to be resilient to get through trials, but yet you have to understand resilience. To be resilient is to be on the defense rather than the offense. To be resilient is the ability to bounce back after every throwback. It gives the image of someone falling down and being able to stand back up. This is a good quality and it is necessary. The part we need to realize is that we can't settle into living on the defense. You need to force yourself to be on the offense, as well. Instead of putting up with the trials that come at us and recovering from them, we need to force ourselves into forward motion at all cost. To be on the offense means moving forward and not giving a second thought to what or who is pushing us back. Being on the offense means being a little bit selfish and in doing so others can get pushed back and hurt by it. There is a balance between willingly hurting others and protecting yourself. Never willingly hurt another person for your own gain, but protect yourself from situations and people trying to hurt you. Living life on the defense is taking the pain and getting through it.

The balance and understanding of resilience is to move forward, have the ability to bounce back but yet you need to strive to live in the offense more than the defense. Live life to conquer strongholds. I keep the mindset of adapt and conquer. Always adapt to the situations and conquer oppositions and you will get far. Wisdom will come in time as you face trials. When situations in life present we won't have all of the answers on how to get through them or how to push forward. There is a certain level to where we need the knowledge to know our resources to get through to the end. Wisdom does not mean having all of the answers or knowing how to get through the situation you are in, but it does mean admitting you don't know how and having the knowledge to find the resources that will allow you to succeed.

Chapter 19

Forgiveness

For many years I struggled with forgiveness. Forgiving those who hurt me was a hard pill for me to swallow. I had been taught in church growing up that we are to forgive those who do wrong to us because the example in the bible is the ultimate forgiveness that Jesus gave his life on the cross so that we could all be forgiven. This is the basic truth that I do base my faith on. I have accepted God's forgiveness in my life for all that I personally have done and the things that I will do wrong. The part that I struggled with was being able to have that same heart to forgive others. The idea of turning the other cheek always left me open for more hurt. I learned to forgive my perpetrators during the act of what they were doing to me. I would visualize them as being hurting individuals who were just taking the pains of their life out on me. I would take the abuse from them thinking that I was their means of feeling better about themselves. In those situations, that is what got me through. Today I see that forgiveness is a state of the heart. I believe forgiveness is not a one-time deal. I don't believe that you can just say that you forgive someone and then move on. I believe that forgiveness is a choice and it has to be made daily and on every encounter with the person who hurt you. Forgiveness does not mean allowing yourself to be hurt either. If you are in a bad position where you are being put in harms way, then you need to get out of that situation. People tend to say that if you forgive someone you allow them back into your life. I don't believe that is true.

I learned that lesson only recently. I had forgiven my adopted mother many times for the things she has done wrong in my life. I finally allowed her back into my life when I filed for divorce from my husband and moved out. I contacted her and let her know what was going on and that I needed a support system and I wanted her to be a part of my life again. I brought her to my new home updated her on what had been going on in my life and was excited to have a mother figure back in the picture. She promised to keep my secrets and not let anyone know where I lived. She said that she would be there for me regardless of how the marriage ended. She said that she would miss my husband but told me I came first. I later learned that there were messages back and forth between her and my ex-husband about all the new details in my life. She told him that she was on his side and was sorry that he was hurting. She told him that I would be alone sitting on a couch someday because I will never have anyone else in my life willing to love me. She also told him that she didn't understand how his mother put up with me as a daughter in law because if it were opposite, she would want to kill the girl that made her son so unhappy. Reading that and the other negative things from the woman I allowed back in my life as a mother was devastating.

The conversations between them went on and on for days. At that point I was reminded of the reasons I removed her from my life in the first place. I stopped contact with her and made her aware that she was no longer allowed in my life. I have since forgiven her. While I cannot allow her in my life again to continue to hurt me, I acknowledge the good roles she played at times in my life. I recognize also the damages that will be caused if I continue to allow her back in. We don't have a delete button in our memories. We cannot erase the things that happened with us. They will always be in our minds and we cannot ever forget about them. The choice to continually choose to say that you have forgiven that person each time that memory is brought up is a personal choice that never has an ending.

There are many people in my life who have hurt me and I have to choose each day that I have flashbacks or memories come back into play to forgive them. The hardest part is forgiving someone when they are not sorry because they don't feel like they did anything wrong. Most people I write about in my book won't even admit to themselves that the things they put me through were wrong. Many of them still deny that these things happened or that they were necessarily even though they were wrong. I have to make the choice to forgive them even when they feel they have nothing to be forgiven for. That mindset of forgiveness will take the heaviness off my heart so that I can move past it. It has been said that love is a choice and I strongly believe that statement, as well. In the same mindset, I believe that forgiveness also is a choice. I also believe that it is a requirement to be able to move on in life in peace. There are people who I have told my story to that tell me that I have the right to hold a grudge and never forgive my family. I believe that if I held to that freedom of holding a grudge I would just harbor bitterness. Forgiveness is loving someone who is not loveable. It seems impossible at times but it is necessary for healing.

When this book is published and you are reading it, I will be facing new issues from family members whose names have been covered up. After this is published, the stories will now become public knowledge. You as the reader will not know of whom I am exactly writing but as they read it, they will feel a sense of guilt and any relationship I have built back up with them through forgiveness I can expect to be broken. The people I am writing about will know who they are in the story. Things in my life will fall apart again. I believe that new areas of growth will begin also. That does not mean that the people whom I have written about are not forgiven. I still hold to my heart of forgiveness but again that shows that forgiveness is a two-part decision. Forgiveness is just as difficult received as it is given.

Chapter 20

Guilt and SANE

All of my life, I have been taught through church and from the major portion of my community that surrounded me that women are supposed to be under or submit to their husbands or to the men who are in leadership over them. I do acknowledge that biblically the men are said to be strong, loving, and protecting and their wife is supposed to submit and follow their lead. It can make sense and it feels like a safe way for a woman to live. I can't say that I agree with it as a set standard. By nature women want to be loved and protected. Biblically that is listed as the man's role towards the woman. I have found myself in a battle with that mindset stemming back to my childhood. Since I was a young girl I was forced to submit to the men in authority over me and the things that they did to me as a result of forcibly submitting were wrong and permanently damaging.

After months of struggling in various relationships, hours of counseling, and numerous sleepless nights, it finally clicked where my "disconnect" was. In order to survive throughout my childhood and the teenage years following, I had to figure out a way to protect myself. I had spent so much time submitting to the male leaders in order to survive, and in doing so I allowed myself to be hurt and taken advantage of by them. When I look at what finally allowed me to break away and protect myself, it always came down to me eventually rebelling against the male leaders in my life and running away in order to keep myself safe. I have found that has crossed over into my intimate relationships today. Looking back I can see on my end in different areas the way it contributed to problems that I had in my marriage. I'm not justifying how my husband treated me in the marriage but I am admitting that I played into it with my lack of submission. It is hard for me to submit to the authority of a male figure. I've been telling myself for years that that is what I want and need in my life: A male leader who can guide me and love me unconditionally. I even convinced myself that I really believed that. In concept that is a good thought. In a normal healthy situation that type of structure may be a good thing as long as the structure is set up right and fair to both sides. I've actually been convincing myself that I am still searching for that type of structure. I have found that as I get closer to that structure I have convinced myself so long that I needed, I get scared and I go into self-protection mode. Ultimately, I end up running away to protect myself. That is the only way of life that I've learned to cope in. Constant survival mode is the mode I live in everyday. I'm not saying that that is normal and I am certainly not saying that it is healthy, but I am admitting that that is how I cope.

Sometimes I wonder if I can ever have a normal relationship with a man. Not being able to listen to someone else or having the nature to rebel or run from the male-leader situation is detrimental to the male who is head of the household who needs to be respected at a certain level. I have definitely learned to stand my ground. I will never place myself in a situation again where I will be dominated. There is something to be said of equality and an equal playing field. On my part, I can definitely say that there are some simple mistakes I made in the situations I was in during the past that caused permanent damage today. For so many years I've been silent about the things that happened to me and that was my first mistake. I submitted unwillingly to the male figures in my life who hurt me and I kept silent about it. By submitting and not speaking out I felt I was giving consent in a way. Again I blamed myself.

After I became a registered nurse, I took the SANE course. That course allows nurses to become certified as a sexual assault nurse examiner. That was a course that I have wanted to take since I started nursing school. It was a goal of mine to become certified and trained to help others who are in the same sexual assault situations that I have been through myself. Through taking that course, I learned specific definitions of what sexual assault really was. While taking that course, I was thrown into flashback mode and images and scenes came back that I had convinced myself through the years I had gotten over and thought I already dealt with. In those moments it was affirmed to me that as much as I tried to downplay it those events that happened to me were in fact sexual abuse. Sitting in the class watching the videos and hearing the stories made me unable to sit still. Being forced to remember the days that my brothers would explore my body and "go down" on me and place objects inside of me as part of a game caused me to come to the realization that each event was a separate occurrence of sexual abuse and that it was chronic for me. I was re-living the trauma all over again.

In that course I learned about the court system and about pressing charges. I learned about how that all worked. I heard stories of people who have been punished after doing what they did to children. I remember when I was young I thought that my brothers were just playing games with me and in all honesty what was going on did feel good. That type of stimulation in any human being is supposed to feel good because it is a human sexual response. I didn't know better at the time so I didn't stop it or say anything to anyone. When I was 15 and living with my stepfather, I didn't say anything about the things he did to me behind closed doors because I was afraid of hurting my adopted mother if she found out. I didn't want to cause her any more hurt on top of the depression she was going through. If I said something about what he was doing to me and he got in trouble, then I feared that my adopted mother wouldn't have anyone to take care of her or pay her bills. She would beg me to stay with her and not leave her alone with them. I was afraid that she would suffer because of it and it would be my fault. I also felt that no one would believe me even if I did say something. He came across as such a good person and did all the things that normal people would do. He was active in extracurricular activities and church. The family had no idea about the things I was going through. Even the things I told them no one except one of my stepfather's sisters believed until the day his own daughter came out and admitted that he did inappropriate things to her, as well. At that point, people believed what I had told them. At that point, it was also too late for me to be heard. Now that the statute of limitations has passed for me to press charges and prosecute, I have this lingering sense of guilt. Now I still wonder if my stepfather is going to engage in the same behavior with other girls or if my stepbrothers will harm other innocent people in the same way they would torment me. Most of all I worry if my adopted brother will continue to molest other little girls.

What has really concerned me is something that happened when my oldest adopted brother who had done the most harm to me came back to Michigan after working for the carnival. He got a mentally handicapped woman pregnant. When she had a baby girl, no one suspected that he was sexually abusing her until she turned seven years old and told people that her daddy was hurting her and that he would use scissors inside of her. People didn't believe her stories because she was considered mentally incompetent, as well. I was distraught when charges were brought up warrants were put out for his arrest but no justice was brought to the matter because no one has seen him or heard from him in years. For all we know he's still out working for the carnival and will never return to Michigan. I still live with the thought every day that it is my fault that his daughter went through the same things he put me through. My lack of saying something at the appropriate time caused another little girl, and possibly others from what I've heard recently, to be harmed sexually, physically and emotionally by him. Those people will all be scarred for the rest of their lives like I am. It is hard to not take that guilt upon myself everyday.

My hope is that through taking this course and becoming certified to assist women in their moments of victimization, I will be able to encourage them, empower them and give them hope and strength. I personally know how hard it is to make a decision to press charges. I now understand the results and the guilt that comes from not doing so. For anyone who is in that situation and is on the fence about pressing charges, I would encourage you to move forward and bring justice to those who have been hurt or the ones who will be hurt next. The world is a scary place. Understandably, it is not something most people want to spend a lot of time thinking about. Abuse comes in all forms and happens where you would least expect it. Victims of abuse have many issues and the way they live life tends to be altered because of it. People see the way they live and pass judgment yet no one knows the reasons behind their behavior and quirks.

The statistics are staggering: 17.7 million Americans have been sexually assaulted, 15% of them were under the age of 12 when it happened. Add to that the knowledge that sexual assault is one of the most unreported crimes and it's pretty disturbing. But it's not something anyone wants to dwell on so we don't talk about it. When we hear a statistic stating 1 in 6 women will endure sexual assault, we say to ourselves those are someone else's friends. Maybe we assume that people in poverty or of a different race deal with this more than we do and that it couldn't be anyone we know. Whoever you are, you know someone who has been sexually assaulted.

Victims of sexual assault are three times more likely to suffer from depression. They are 6 times more likely to suffer from post-traumatic stress disorder, 13 times more likely to abuse alcohol, 26 times more likely to abuse drugs and four times more likely to contemplate suicide. But some of them rise above. Some of them decide that after surviving that they are going to live the best life they could live and God help anyone who tries to stop them.

As a survivor, I can relate when it comes to the feeling of losing yourself and your identity after being a victim. I struggled for a long time with the fact that I was worthless and that I was violated and unworthy of real love. I kept trying to get back to the person I used to be. I wasn't sure who I really was. I wanted to be "normal" again. I wanted to get to the point where I didn't have the flashbacks or memories every time I was touched or saw something that brought me back to a bad place in my life. I had to realize that the things I went through were a part of my story and have shaped me into who I am today. I will never get back to being the person that I was. You can never change the situations in your past, but you can change who you become in your future. If I allow the thoughts and hopes of getting back to who I was creep in all the time, then I will remain stagnant and I won't go anywhere in life. What has happened in the past happened and there is no going back to take it away. It can define you if you let it, but it doesn't have to. I use my bad situations to help others and I feel honored to do so. It creates strength and confidence when channeled in the right direction. It is sad that bad things happen in the world. Good people make the bad situations tolerable and strong people create a state of confidence and character. If you are struggling with getting back to where you were, take a moment to reframe, allow the past to settle and use it in your future to empower others to get through it. Give your past purpose.

Chapter 21

Conquering Predestination

There is a particular stigma that goes along with children that grew up like I did. There's an expectation of failure immediately. It is true that people in my situation who face the same trials that I have faced typically tend to have low self-esteem, lower employment rates and poor outcomes in life. That is a simple statistics and a fact proven by surveys. Through my experience and resilience, I now truly believe that it is possible to beat those statistics. Defeating a statistic is simply done by making the numbers higher on the positive end than those you are fighting against. With enough resilient people beating the odds, that negative statistic can become a hopeful one. My life gave me an outline that if I had followed the typical path, I would have ended up back on the streets where I started. With my biker father and prostitute mother, I would have been a negative statistic if I stayed in the rut I was born into. I may have never acquired my career. I may never have found happiness or contentment and I would still be struggling to find enough food to eat. Who knows if I would even still be alive now. I could be a prostitute or drug dealer, and I could have very well been in the same van as my brother when he was murdered.

Overall, without an inward determination of resilience, things would look a lot different now. As my life story was being written for me according to what was predestined to happen, I took the pen back. I decided that my life was not going to go the way that everyone expected it would go. I overcame obstacles and I persevered through the hard times. I kept my eyes focused on what was ahead and I kept hope in my heart. I knew that God had a bigger plan and purpose for my life and that it was possible for me to succeed. I knew that everything that I have been through was for a purpose. I knew deep inside that someday I would somehow help others. Keeping that goal in mind pushed me forward and gave my life purpose. The sense of helping others who struggled as I did and continuing to move forward while not looking back at the past was what allowed me to get to where I am now. I didn't end up on the streets in the end. I spent some time there and I learned a lot about life. I decided that that wasn't going to be my life. Your final destination is all about your choice. You have the choice to be where you want to be in life. The typical ending of the life you are born into should not cloud your view of where you are able to end up. If I wanted to stay in the streets I could have. I had friends there; I had the hook ups and the connections to make it just fine living on the streets. I could make it through each day just fine and get by in everyday life and just barely make it by leaning on friends and the people that would appear in my path. It was always an option to rely on getting help from others. I decided I wasn't going to stand around taking hand outs to get by. I chose to be one that is able to give help. I went from being someone who is needy to someone who helps the needy. I made that a goal. There were times when I needed the help and I took it when I had to. Now is the time that I'm finally able to be the one to help. Who you were yesterday does not make you who you are today. I was able to learn that lesson in life. Just because my past told me that I was supposed and up in a certain way in the future did not mean that that I was going to let that happen.

Each day you get to choose who you are. We get the choice to be who we want to be in life and do what we want to do. We have the option to write our own life story. If we want to have a life that is sad, poor and hopeless we will have that. If that's really what you want, you will have it. You can get whatever you want out of life. You just have to want it. It's a question of how bad you really want it. We can't blame the past for the person we are becoming. Tomorrow does not have to be defined by the past. Tomorrow is a new day and we have the potential to be a new person. I chose to become a new person. I chose to not let my destiny that was given to me at birth predestinate my future. It is a simple matter of choosing to say "how?" instead of asking "why?" In the moments in life when you feel as though you're being tested, don't look up and ask "why?" Just simply say "how?"

The first step is looking inside and deciding whether or not you should have studied for this test. For a test you take in a class, you need to study in order to pass. You won't pass the test without studying unless you're really lucky. Some people do get lucky in life. Some people do get a lot of handouts. They get to pass the test without studying and putting in the effort. Good for them. It isn't a bad thing on their part. It is just a different lot in life they were given. Your "grade" at the end of the "class" is dependent on how much you study and how much you put into it. With life's tests you have to prepare. You have to be ready and you have to try your hardest. No one else can take the test for you and no one else can study for you. It will all pay off in the end when you get your "degree" and you finally become something in life. Someone said to me one time "just because everything points to that doesn't mean it has to end in that." I took from that saying everything I just wrote about in this chapter. Your life doesn't have to end in the situation in which it began.

In life we face trials daily. I learned by going into a workplace where I was intimidated by everyone and all the tasks ahead of me, that this was only a part of my life. I look at the life I have lived and the trials I have faced and I remind myself of the ways I have defeated trials. I place that confidence on every other situation in my life. When I walk into that workplace, I ask myself "What could possibly happen here in this building that I have not already faced in life?" I have conquered bigger trials in my life than anything a day at work can throw at me. When I go into an interview, what is the worst thing that can happen? This is the mindset that keeps me confident. Remembering your accomplishments allows you to move forward in confidence even in the midst of defeat.

I always look at the worst-case scenario in any situation I find myself. I acknowledge it and I realize there is always a best case scenario and a worst case scenario. I go through in my mind how things can end up for the worst and I come up with a plan on how to handle the worst case. Once I have a back up plan and a way to get through the worst-case scenario, I have now defeated it and it can no longer be worst case anymore. This is essential to life. We have to acknowledge the fact that things will not always be easy. When we acknowledge that and defeat it with a backup plan, there isn't much that can deter us from success. Always have a solution for the worst-case scenario and it will only get easier from there. Don't ever let people bring you down. You will come to meet many people who stand in your way and many who will make your life difficult. I look at this in a way that allows me to see the bigger picture. Looking at it in the life story point of view, I see that each person has a life story. In each person's life story, there are different characters that come in and out. Some play bigger roles and some play minimal ones but still make it onto a page. If someone in your path is bringing you down, stop and ask yourself a question. Ask yourself "when the story of my life is written, will this person make it into my book?" If the answer to that question is no, then don't even add them in as a footnote. Move forward and know that this is just a person you need to pass by in life to continue on in your story. If you let people play a bigger role in your life than they should, then you have given them the pen to write in your book. When living life, always hold on to the pen that writes your story.

Chapter 22

Health lost to trials faced

The struggles I faced throughout the years put a lot of stress on my body. It can be said and verified that the trials I faced aged me. The average person would not guess that I am only 24 years old. When I ask for people to guess my age, the first guess is always in the high 30's. Stress does a lot of damage to the body and I can understand that on a medical level now that I am a nurse. I have had numerous cardiac tests done and have been placed on various medications for stress, anxiety and depression. I refused the cardiac medications or the thyroid medications because I believed that the levels that they were correcting were only temporary due to my stressful living situation during my struggles in life. I not only look older than my age but I feel older, too. The normal things that a 24-year-old woman would be doing would include staying out late at night with friends. I can't even stay up past 9 pm without trying not to fall asleep during a conversation. I have no energy to do the things that I used to do. I get fatigued easily. My heart races at random times and I sometimes have fainting episodes after my heart goes into SVT (this is a condition where the heart rate goes straight from 80 beats per minute into the 200 beat per minute range and won't slow down). I cannot control when this happens and I have the fear that I am going to go into cardiac arrest every time it happens. It is a scary condition and I have watched many people in the ER I work in come in with this, sometimes with fatal results.

The fact that I survived a traumatic brain injury gives me struggles to face, as well. I now have a hard time converting things from short term to long-term memory. I remember everything before the accident without a problem but any new information I have to write down otherwise I will forget it. The neurologists say that this can be temporary or permanent and that only time will tell as the years go by. My friends who were around me at the time of the accident can understand why I have memory issues. It is hard to explain to new people that I meet the reason I have to ask their name each time we hang out. It is hard to explain the reason that I introduce the same two people over and over again. I am very thankful to be alive from that accident but that is a valid concern that I face daily now. I have a hard time hearing out of my right ear from the accident and I have to ask people to repeat things a lot. That is also frustrating at 24 years old! The trigeminal neuralgia that I have as an effect from the accident can cause the right side of my face to randomly go numb because of the nerve damage. My eyesight is even affected as a residual effect from the brain injury. I have moments where my mind goes blank and I just stare into space and I can't process things or make conversation because my mind just shuts off. It is like there is a curtain between my thoughts. I can't think past it. These are all things I have taken for granted but I understand that they are all health gifts that not all are fortunate to have and I don't want to waste the blessing while I have it.

With every headache I get as a result of the head injury, I am suddenly put back into my place and I am reminded how short and precious life is. I am at risk of a stroke at any time now and I have to be careful not to hit my head on anything. With the headaches I get now, the pain intensifies with each beat of my heart. I always pray that God sustains me through the painful migraines. These are all mild concerns in exchange for the opportunity I have to take each single breath I am blessed with. I am reminded daily that life is sacred and that I was a fool to ever even think of taking my own life willingly despite how bad life became.

Chapter 23

Happiness follows you

People always ask me how I can be so happy when things in my life are not going well. What they are talking about is my countenance or demeanor. How you present yourself on the outside is how people perceive you regardless of how you feel on the inside. When I think about it, happiness is a state of mind and happiness is also your choice. Throughout everything I have been through, I have chosen to find happiness. Things have not always been easy for me. Things in my life have been the exact opposite of easy. Regardless, I choose to smile and keep my chin up and then to everyone around me, my countenance is bright. When people see your smiling face, they feel welcome. When you give off warmth, you are inviting people to come over and talk to you. If you need something and if you are positive then people will be more willing to help you out. People tend to steer clear of people with a sad face or people who look like they don't want to be talked to because they are depressed. No one wants to talk to someone who is sinking into his or her own dark place. Those types of people generally feel sorry for themselves and don't want anyone to know that they're hurting. I was there once, and I got nowhere but deeper into depression because I didn't understand why people didn't care that I was hurting.

Part of the process of becoming resilient is knowing when to ask for help. A big part is admitting that sometimes you do actually need help. You need to be self-motivated to make things happen on your own but you also need to realize that you can't do everything on your own. There have been times in my life when I have received a helping hand from people and people have felt sorry for me and helped me out. Although I don't like being felt sorry for, I realize that there were points that I really needed help and I didn't have the resources to help myself. If I would not have been bright and hopeful and if I didn't still manage to carry a smile, people would have steered away from me. Those people would not have taken the time to get to know me or to come over to ask my name. Having a smile on my face is the first thing that I could do to help myself. No one will help you if you are not willing to help yourself because then it would be pointless and you wouldn't go anywhere. If you are happy in your life, happiness will follow you. If you're sad the same goes. If you are sad, sadness will follow you. If you run away from your problems and you never found happiness in the first place, you won't find happiness the next place you went because you didn't take it with you. The next place you end up will look different around you but the key player that hasn't changed is yourself. If you're sad and you're down on life nothing will change that unless you decide to change it yourself. Your situations or your circumstances will change, but you will not. Whatever you have inside you and whatever you tell yourself you are, that is what would follow you and that is what shows. If you want to see a positive change in your life, you have to be the positive change in your life.

A friend once told me that when he goes on the golf course, he dresses up really nice and he looks good. Even if he's tired, he smiles because if he looks good, he feels good and then he plays good. He explained to me the look good, feel good, play good model. It all begins when you get up in the morning and you prepare for your day. I have tried to apply that model in my own life. When I get up in the morning, I have a choice. I can be happy today or I can realize that my current situation sucks and I can have a depressed mindset. I realize that being sad keeps me at home. It makes me unwilling to go out and it makes me unwilling to respond to text messages. It forces me to stay home because I don't look good. When I don't look good, I don't feel good and therefore I know I'm not going to play good. So I found that even if my night was a terrible night when I went to sleep. I wake up in the morning and realize it's a new day. Situations may be the same today as they were yesterday but today I can be different.

I do my best to put on a smile to make myself presentable to make it appear as though nothing is going wrong and then I smile and I walk out the door and my day is instantly a better day. People are warmly welcomed by me so they come up and talk to me. When people approach me to talk to me, it encourages me. I then start to feel worth and happiness. If I would have left the house in a bad mood realizing that my life is not going the way I want it to, then I would have a sad face walking out the door and no one would approach me. I would be down and it would be contagious. People would be scared to talk to me and no one would want to ask me what is wrong.

Truth be told, it scares people to know that someone's hurting. If you know someone is upset then you feel obligated to take the time to listen and help. It is the idea of passing by a stranger and casually saying "how are you" and continuing to walk forward. That phrase is thrown out everyday. No one who says those words to you in passing is really expecting you to take the time to sit down and tell them how you really are doing. With care and concern comes time and investment. I try not to say that phrase to people casually unless I really have the time to find out how that person is really doing and to take the time to listen. Everyone has a story and everyone has problems. The difference between different people is how they carry themselves on the outside despite how they are feeling on the inside. If I am depressed, I put on a smile to encourage someone else. When they talk to me and tell me what is going on in their life, I can encourage them. By doing so I am then encouraged and I feel better about myself because I know that I was able to help another person.

The key message to this again is that if you're happy,

happiness will follow you, if you are sad, then sadness will follow you. The first step to getting help and admitting that you need help is to just smile and attempt to be happy. Stop feeling sorry for yourself and just smile and realize that that is your first step to helping yourself look good, feel good and play good. This doesn't mean that you should pretend nothing is wrong and bury your problems and just never deal with them. The point is that if you are hopeful and carry yourself in a positive manner, then help will come to you and you will finally be able to work through your problems.

A pianist friend of mine shared his thoughts of how the show must go on. I had been hanging out with a lot of musicians lately. Musicians, I would say, are in the category of artists. And respectfully speaking I would have to say that they are their own breed. This is a good thing. Artists and musicians think outside the box and are more colorful than most people think. They perceive things in many different ways as opposed to having one view. A phrase I learned from this pianist is "the show must go on." He spoke those words to me after he heard what I was struggling with in life. He told me that regardless of anything I face, I must continue to move forward. He gave the analogy of when he goes on to perform. He steps backstage and is getting ready to go in front of an audience of thousands. He has been preparing for months for the show and people have invested a lot of money into seeing the production. Regardless of what has happened that day or that week in his life, he has a duty to the audience that follows him. He related this to my life. In life, I have a duty and a purpose. I actually believe that. There are many people to whom I give advice and mentor and there are many people who I look up to in the same way.

When a leader struggles, you would never know it because they work through it until the show is over. When it comes time in life for my show to go on, I have to remember that anything bad that has happened during the day, in the past week or in my life cannot hold me back from the performance of life. Life is our show and each day is a new production. Society is the audience. We cannot cancel a show that people are waiting to take part in because we had a bad day. Life happens. People ask me how I can get up and walk again after being thrown down so many times. I now tell them "the show must go on." Life will not stop. Sometimes it ends, and sometimes it's harder than others. Life doesn't just stop. If we stop, your life will continue on without you and you will become stagnant. We need to keep moving forward. Progress is progress. Even if that means one step a day, you still need to take that step. Any step in the forward direction is better than remaining where you were. When you are about to allow your situations to affect your decisions, that is where you need to step back and realize the production is much bigger and there's more behind the scenes that goes on but yet, the show must go on.

Chapter 24

Trauma hurts

In life, some people like to play the game of comparisons. By nature, people want sympathy and compassion. It is easy to feel like your pain is more valid than the pain others feel. Some people tend to think that no one can hurt as bad as they do and that no one could have ever gone through what they have gone through. This is in fact the farthest from the truth. An example would be people living with post traumatic stress disorder (PTSD). A combat veteran who comes back from war who just lost many friends in an explosion now has to deal with the flashbacks and the memories rushing back in every time they hear fireworks or a loud noise. I went to Disney world with a friend who recently came back on medical leave from Iraq. As soon as the fireworks started going off, he jumped into the bushes. This is not a funny thing. He was instantly sent back into a war setting. His fear came back and his adrenaline couldn't stop. He was scared and confused and his first response was to run for cover. This type of thing happens constantly to people all around you and they have to try to fit into society or walk through a crowd and try to avoid a panic attack. A flashback brings back instant fear and it puts you right back to where the memory occurred. The pain all comes back at once and it's one of the worst feelings ever. The flashbacks are hard to deal with everyday, and there isn't a particular medication that can stop flashbacks. They are a part of life that people who suffer with them have to learn to deal with.

The pain of a person who struggles with PTSD from a war setting is similar to the trauma suffered when I was out with my friends at a street race at night in Detroit. I watched my best friend get shot in the forehead right next to me. At the time it happened, I went into shock. As the shooter turned and ran away, my friends picked me up and threw me into their car to get away from the scene. There were many gunshots going back and forth through the incident. Now every time that I hear gunshots or fireworks, I automatically go into flashback mode. Over time, I have dealt with it to the point where I can hear the noise and maintain composure on the outside. Inside, the memories of that night are still present and my heart will still race. No one would know by just looking at me how much I am struggling in my mind. I get taken back to the place where I remember my best friend getting shot and killed right in front of me. That pain is no different than the flashback that the combat veteran goes through. People tend to think that PTSD only affects veterans. People think that there are different levels of PTSD that make one person hurt worse than another. The pain is the same. Anyone who has experienced a flashback will understand the level of trauma involved. Physical trauma hurts. Emotional trauma doesn't stop. No one would've expected that such a young girl would have lost a friend in such a tragic manner. No one would be able to look at her and see her pain or understand what she is going through on the inside. I now relate this gunshot to that tragic event. Any time I hear a loud noise I will be transported right back to the feelings and events at the original occurrence. The same goes with the veteran. It is an instant flashback of the war setting. I have an ingrained fear now that it is possible for me to lose the people closest to me at any given moment in any situation. Bad things do happen and you can never prepare for them.

My biological father would have never expected to watch his own son get shot right in front of him. Now he deals with the same flashbacks with any loud noise he hears, as well. To him, the pain of losing his son comes back to him again. The combat veteran has his own battles, yet they each hurt the same. No one's pain is greater than another. It is just handled differently. Emotional scars are worse than physical scars because no one knows that they are there. In those cases it is easy to have your emotions get swept under the rug. The people hurting are the last ones to speak out. I personally never talk about the flashbacks I experience. I just move forward. I compose myself and get through the situation.

What needs to happen is for people to reach out to support groups and build community. Support goes two ways. You need to be a source of support yourself and be willing to help others. Even if you've been hurt, you have to be willing to help the hurting. Otherwise, your hurt would have been for nothing. Community and support are what makes life worth living. It makes life possible to move forward in. It gives us strength to move toward the next day. That is the difference between a person getting counseling and the one who commits suicide. I personally lost many friends to suicide. I have come close myself. Looking back in each situation, the ones that I held dearest to me that are now gone, I always wondered if there was something more I could have done. I wonder if there was something I could have said or just something that could have changed the outcome. It is not just one person who affects a life that is lost. It is a combination of many people. I have talked to suicide survivors and people who were on their way to commit suicide but stopped. Some people who were headed to end their life changed their mind because of a positive person they ran into on the way.

I remember the day that I went to the store to get supplies to end my life. While I was checking out, I was happy. I finally felt that the emotional pain I was going through was going to be over and I wouldn't have to suffer anymore. As the bagger put my items in my bag she said to me "I wish I had your smile, you are going to change a lot of lives with that smile never lose it!" I got into the car and shut the door. I felt like every person I passed knew what I was about to do. As I placed my bag on the passenger side floor I thought about what that person just said to me. I was reminded that my suffering had a purpose and I was supposed to help people and be a positive change. I was then reminded that I was counted worthy to suffer. As I drove back to the place I was staying, I changed my mindset. I decided that I could not end my life because then the trials I faced in the route would have been pointless.

There's a saying I have heard: "be kinder than necessary to everyone you meet because everyone's you meet is also facing some sort of battle." That is a very true saying. You never know what someone's dealing with in his or her life. Sometimes we walk past a person in a hurry or when you cut off a person in traffic and look over and give them a mean look to try and prove a point. Sometimes there is the person we angrily rush around with a shopping cart in the store. When we are in these scenarios, we are passing a person who is facing many struggles. Everyone has a story. Don't walk around in life thinking that yours is the only one that matters or that no one else has a story to tell. Be willing to reach out and to comfort one another. Also be willing to tell people when you hurt. If you never open up, they will never know you are hurting. Then it will only be your secret and your pain will only grow deeper. Everyone needs an outlet and everyone needs someone they can trust. Be trustworthy and learn to be trusting. Be open and reach out. Even if you are hurting, know that you are not the only one. Remember that you can be the last person that touches someone's life at the right moment

Chapter 25

Facing Death

There have been many close calls with fate in my life. I have tasted death more times than I would like. Each time I have survived has been a miracle. When I tell people these stories, they look at me like I'm crazy or like I am a ghost because I should not have lived through them. I have ridden motorcycles and dirt bikes the past seven years of my life. On my first street motorcycle, which would be known in the biker world as a crotch rocket, I was following a group of bikers and street racing cars into a parking lot that had gravel and construction cones at the entrance of the driveway. This was only the first week of me riding. I had just learned to ride the weekend prior. I did not realize that they were turning into that driveway. I quickly hit my brakes and I turned left into the driveway of the collision shop where they were meeting. As I turned, my tires hit the gravel, my bike went down and slid across the pavement, and I went rolling across the pavement into oncoming traffic. I was picked up off the road by one of the guys who were there and put into the back of a pick-up truck. The cops came, and my bike was towed away. The people I was with took me away as the cops came to avoid any trouble or questions being asked. The people I was with didn't know me well enough to know my insurance situation or accident history so they were looking out for me by avoiding any police contact.

Luckily, I had a helmet on and I was wearing a jacket and blue jeans. My only injuries were road rash from my clothing that was moved as I rolled across the pavement.

Luckily the oncoming traffic saw me and stopped. That bike was totaled. A week later, I did not want to miss the next bike night in downtown Royal Oak so I bought another motorcycle. I rode that new motorcycle for a couple months until I got comfortable and then I decided to take it on a road trip to Chicago with my friend Anna whom I wrote about earlier in the book. She rode on the back with me all the way down. On the way home from Chicago, we had a little mishap. Anna was the passenger on my bike so she was wearing a backpack that held all of our clothing. As we were on the freeway, the zipper to the backpack came undone. I started to feel my bike pulling as we were going 80 mph. I felt something hitting my leg repeatedly. I wasn't sure what was going on. I slowed down and I looked to my left to see that there was a pair of jeans stuck in my motorcycle chain. I pulled over to the side of the freeway.

When we got off the bike we took a closer look at it. The backpack was open and the contents had flown out. The jeans were caught in the chain of my motorcycle. We started picking out shreds of the fabric and removed all of the jean parts that were stuck in the chain. That incident should have killed us. I still to this day cannot believe that we were able to ride with blue jeans stuck in the chain of a moving motorcycle on only two wheels. We both realized how close we came to a bad wreck.

A few months after that incident, I was heading home from the street races in Detroit with my friend Britney on the back of my bike. It was 3 o'clock in the morning. We were on interstate 94 coming Eastbound. All of a sudden, I felt the back of my bike swaying to the left and the right. I nudged Britney and told her to sit down. I thought she was standing up and moving around. I turned around and realized she was sitting down. She gripped me tighter. At that point, I didn't know what was going on but I knew I had to pull over. The closest exit was 8 mile. That was a very unsafe area but I knew that we didn't have a choice and we were going to have to stop. I pulled off the freeway and entered into a gas station. We looked at each other and realized that this was a bad time of night to be where we were. We parked the bike and got off. We went to the back of the bike to look at the back tire and saw that half of the tire was missing. It had shredded off and blown out. I can't even tell you how it was even possible that the bike kept going and didn't throw us off. In that instant we should've died, but yet again I'm alive. In that situation not only did we miraculously survive but the story of that gas station in the bad area was a unique one. A couple of guys walked over to us and asked us what we were doing there so late. They looked at the bike and told us that they would be right back. Out of the gas station walked a tall guy in a black hoody who looked at me and said "hey you are the girl that rode with me and my buddies the other day." I looked at him and said "oh yeah, you are the guy that was on the Repsol." It turns out the guy that owned that gas station was someone I had met a few days earlier when I rode with a random group that I saw the riding on the freeway. That was the culture of riding. If you are riding alone you join up with other riders you see nearby. Then at the next gas stop, you exchange info and gain riding buddies. He brought us inside the store, let us go into the back and told us to get whatever we wanted off the shelves to eat or drink. He loaded up my bike up on the back of his truck and in the morning, when the next person came to the gas station to take over for him, he dropped us off back at Britney's house. He took my bike to a repair shop for me. Talk about divine appointments and God taking care of me.

I had another observation on being taken away a young age when my brother was not. If I would've stayed at home with my brother and biological family in the early stages of my life and not gotten taken to foster care, I may have been with my brother and my biological father the day Brian was murdered. I could also have been killed. There was also the time I should have died in the accident Shauna was in. I was riding in the car with her on the way to our soccer game and I was supposed to get in the same vehicle with her on the way home. I got into the car with my coach instead because he wanted to talk to me about the game and I would've died that day when Shauna died in the accident because that was the car was supposed to be in. There have been many shaky situations that I should not have made it through for putting myself in that situation but yet I made it out okay. The bicycle accident is another example I wrote about already of how I survived a potentially fatal situation.

I have been in one automobile crash in my whole life and it was near fatal. I was on my way to a guitar class. I was at a red light. I rolled down my driver side window to pour out the rest of my coffee and then the light turned green. As I took off, the cars on the left side of the intersection had already stopped for their red light. I crossed over the median and a car coming from the right side of the intersection ran through the red light at 55 mph. The car t-boned me on my passenger side. It shoved the right side of my car into the right side of my body. That crash would have been fatal with my pre-existing skull fracture but seconds before the impact I rolled down my driver side window. The fact that that window was open at that time is what saved my life. I went to the ER and thankfully I was not severely injured. I have some residual effects from the accident, such as right-sided weakness and nerve damage but I'm alive.

I look at that situation and I see God's hand of protection once again. I am not saying that I am invincible but I am saying that I am fully aware that God wants me around for some reason. The night before that particular car crash, I was walking through a park in downtown Detroit. I met a man I talked with for a while. He told me of his life struggles in Detroit and his battles with homelessness. He told me that he saw something in me that made him believe that I am "anointed." He told me that the kingdom of darkness, also known as the devil, does not want me doing what I am planning to do for the Lord. He told me that the way I'm living my life and the purpose that God has for my life is going to cost me a lot of trouble in life. I laughed and told him that I already knew that and I was already well into the trial. He warned me that night to keep my guard up. He was prophesying over me. He told me that someone was going to try to wipe me out so that I couldn't accomplish the greater purpose for my life. He said that I will be okay regardless of what comes at me because I have got divine protection and I have not yet accomplished His purpose. He told me to keep my faith and continue to move forward. That was the night right before the accident I just wrote about.

The next morning while in the hospital, I thought back on those words and I realize what he meant. That was my second reminder of the purpose God has for me and my story in life. I really do believe in divine appointments and divine protection. I realize when I tell people these stories it is hard for them to grasp the faith I gain from these experiences because they are MY experiences. The feeling of being so close to death and wondering if you are really still alive is not something that everyone can experience. I cant convince anyone of my faith with my words, but I can share my story and continue to live my life out because my story tends to speak for itself and I am glad to be a living example of hope. A bit of humor I can add to this is the fact that in my bicycle accident I gained the nickname of squirrel. That name came because the last memory I had before the bike crash was a squirrel. So my friends shout "squirrel" when I walk by at work and it has been a funny joke because I saved a squirrel and cracked my head open. The last car crash I just wrote about actually happened on Squirrel Rd in Auburn Hills, MI. That led to a lot of laughs and humor in the situation.

Chapter 26

Faith

Through the years the people that have told me that I needed to write a book would all tell me that they didn't know how I made it through life as well as I have. People always say that by looking at me now, they would never guess I ever went through any of the things I have been through. As I reflect back, I look at what had held me up and allowed me to persevere through it all. It was my faith. My faith in Christ is the only thing that was consistent all the way through. Many people don't share the same faith as I do or even have faith at all and to those people who don't and are still struggling, all I can suggest is maybe it is time to explore the option of faith. Maybe that is what will finally make the light turn on for you as it did for me.

My personal faith is not in a religion but in the example I learned in the bible long ago. I learned an example of love, forgiveness and grace. My faith is in Jesus Christ. I call myself a Christian, which historically in the translation means 'like Christ.' I look at the examples in the Bible of how Jesus came to earth perfect and did nothing wrong while he was here. What He did was help people. He fed the poor. He hung out with the outcasts and healed the sick. Those are all good things. Regardless of the good that he did he was treated very poorly and he didn't have a place to lay his head at night most nights. I relate to him in that aspect. People told Him that He was wrong for eating and drinking with tax collectors and sinners. He always said that He didn't come to earth for the healthy but rather for the sick. He suffered on this earth to the point of death on the cross in order to take our sins upon himself. He did that so that if we have faith in Him, we will have forgiveness for all we do on earth and then we can have everlasting joy in heaven. This has been my hope.

This is the example of sacrificial love that I live for. This is what gives my life purpose. I relate myself to Jesus. I tell myself that if He can go through all that suffering after doing nothing wrong, then who am I to complain when things go wrong in my life? I have to remember that at any point in time things can always be worse. I live my life to try to love and help people as Jesus did in the bible. That gives me purpose in life and that makes all the suffering I went through worth it because it reminds me that all of it is for a higher purpose.

I have not always been faithful to the Christian life. When I got married, my husband and I stopped going to church. He would tell me to tell our family and friends that we were going to a church in Troy, Michigan to avoid questions and guilt. I fell away from the faith during that time and my whole goal in life was excelling at my job and hanging out with my friends. Through the struggles I went through in my marriage, I began nursing school. There was a girl I went to school with named Autumn. I did not know her but somehow she saw that there was deep struggle in my life. She would invite me to church with her and write me letters of encouragement. I denied her church invitations for over a year. Finally I went to Sunday church a few times and found that I loved the pastor and I actually related to what he was saying. Autumn has played a huge role in my life. I believe she was specifically placed in my class in school at just the right time. She continues to send me letters and encourage me even to this day. My husband did not go with me when I would visit her church and he did not like the fact that I was going. He had no interest in going with me and did not want people to think poorly of him for not going with me. Because of his resentment towards it, I stopped going. That is the time that our marriage continued to decline. The following months as I neared the end of nursing school was the timeframe that my husband told me that he was going to divorce me. I was devastated. At that point I decided it was time to go back to church and look for some hope again. I literally felt like getting a divorce was the worst thing I could do. The vows we made were about to be broken. I felt that I would never be forgiven and that I would always be judged as the wife whose husband divorced her for not measuring up.

Autumn asked me to join her at a women's bible study called Watershed. I chose to go with her. I walked into the church for the woman's bible study. I rode my motorcycle there that day so I held onto my helmet as a comfort. Over 200 women that I didn't know surrounded me. I felt very out of place. I looked for Autumn so that I would have someone to sit with. I later found out she didn't even make it to the bible study that day. They sang songs and gave a scripture message. At the end they said it was time to break up into the small groups to pray together. At that point, I felt out of place and began to believe that I was not worthy to be there and that God did not love me because I was about to commit, in my opinion, one of the biggest sins the bible speaks of by going through a divorce. I knew I needed to get out of there immediately. I decided that church was not for me. I was too far gone. I believed that God had stopped loving me and at this point my life was forever shattered beyond repair.

As people split up into groups to pray, I grabbed my helmet and walked through the doors. As I walked towards the parking lot, I heard a voice behind me. A woman out of breath was yelling "stop." I walked faster to avoid a confrontation or to have to answer to anyone. Again she shouted "you with the helmet, stop!" I turned around and she caught up to me. She began to tell me about how she kept glancing back at me across the room during the bible study and said that she felt that God wanted her to pray for me the whole time. She asked me if I was ok and what was going on in my life because she had never saw me at the bible study before and that she had no idea why she felt led to watch me and pray for me. I was out of words. I didn't understand why she singled me out. The girl to my left told me she just had an abortion and the girl to my right just said her mom died that past week. Why me? I didn't understand why she picked me out of a room full of hurting women.

I began to tell her my story and she prayed over me. She told me that no matter where I am and what I have done with my life that God never stopped loving me. She reaffirmed to me that God has a plan to use me and my struggles and that I needed to just surrender to Him. She reminded me that God never left me. He didn't go anywhere. I was the one who had been running from Him. I created my own guilt. Jesus was waiting for me at the same place I left Him. She told me that He wants to remind me that I was already forgiven and covered by His grace before I even asked. She then introduced herself as the pastor's wife. That was the same pastor who I had enjoyed the preaching of months prior when I tried out the church. I was shocked and I felt more loved than any other point in my life. When we finished talking, I walked out of the church towards my motorcycle. At that moment I fell to the ground in tears. That was the moment that God showed me that even if I felt I was committing the worst sin, He was not going to leave me and that he still loved me. He sent that woman to me specifically to remind me of that. He had never left me. He had kept me safe through my childhood years in situations I should have never been in and He still showed me how much he cared even to that point. That was the moment when I knew that I was going to be ok. It was the moment I finally accepted God's love and forgiveness. That was the moment that I was reminded that the only thing constant that brought me through all my trials in life was God and His protection, plan and purpose.

For me, that is just one story of how God has shown His presence in my life. I was reminded of that again shortly after when I started to doubt and get depressed again when I got in the bicycle accident. After meeting with a

Neurophysicist who told me that my level of functioning is unheard of after that accident, I was able to acknowledge the fact that God does miracles and is the Ultimate Healer. To this day the signs just keep lighting up for me and I am constantly reminded that I really am here for a purpose. Sometimes it takes rough times to see the greater purpose but sometimes people's eyes are opened to that fact before the trials come. For me, there is no way I can doubt that there is a God because there has been too much evidence of His presence in my life. I can say without a doubt that the suffering was worth it all for that reason alone. Now I have hope in that. In order to help others and to live intentionally to share my story of how God can use you no mater how broken you are and that your life has a specific purpose no matter how many scars you may have. Without scars, you have no story to tell. People with a perfect life are not able to empathize with people who have been hurt. It simply doesn't work. They may be able to sympathize but not personally from being in that situation. I used to laugh at people when they tried to help me through things. I always thought there was no way that they will be able to understand or help. It is the people with a similar story to mine who have seen the horrors of the world that need to step up and acknowledge the hurt instead of hiding it. When the hurt is hidden, it is pointless and it was all for nothing. When we acknowledge it and use our story of trials to help someone else, then we can finally heal because there will be no true healing without seeing the higher purpose behind our story.

What I just gave was a minimal timeline of the key events of my life. Within that outline are stories that endure - stories of wisdom, hope, encouragement and reality. The stories I shared are the purpose of this book. This book is not to complain about my life but to give an overview of understanding the general timeline and the resilience that can be obtained through the bullet points that lie within the timeline of my sufferings. I hope that you can be encouraged to share your story. Your story does matter. You are significant and your trials that you have defeated will give others strength and hope to endure through theirs. Time does heal. The biggest part of the healing process is wanting to stand back up after you fall. In order to move forward past trials in life we have to WANT to move forward. It may be comforting to sit and cry and it feels good to have sympathy. Sympathy is good, but it is also temporary. It is healthy to cry and I am not opposed to crying. I honestly wish I had the ability to cry more to avoid the strain of the tears being held in unwillingly. The pain of not being able to cry when you know you need to is harder than crying in public. The throat gets tight, the headache begins, the eyes water but nothing comes out. If you are able to cry through your trials, at some point you will cry your last tear. At that point, you get the chance to be resilient. At that point you are given the choice to stand back up knowing that falling is only a part of the process. When you reach that point, you will be unstoppable.

FOLLOW UP

If you would like to contact the author to ask questions or to provide feedback or to even share your own story please feel free to e-mail Rachel at F4ischer@gmail.com If you have suggestions about people or groups to whom this book may impact please send an email with your comments and suggestions.

Made in the USA
Charleston, SC
27 October 2013